D1626119

The River Cottage

Preserves Handbook

The River Cottage
Preserves Handbook

by Pam Corbin

introduced by

Hugh Fearnley-Whittingstall

www.rivercottage.net

BLOOMSBURY

LONDON · OXFORD · NEW YORK · NEW DELHI · SYDNEY

for my daughters
Pip and Maddy

First published in Great Britain 2008

Text © 2008 by Pam Corbin
Photography © 2008 by Gavin Kingcome
Additional photography © 2008 by Lois Wakeman

The beech noyau recipe on p.138 is reprinted by permission
of HarperCollins Publishers Ltd © Richard Mabey, 1972

The moral right of the author has been asserted.

Bloomsbury Publishing Plc, 50 Bedford Square, London WC1B 3DP

www.bloomsbury.com

Bloomsbury is a trademark of Bloomsbury Publishing Plc
Bloomsbury Publishing, London, Oxford, New York, New Delhi and Sydney

A CIP catalogue record for this book is available from the British Library.

ISBN 978 0 7475 9532 8
20 19 18 17 16 15 14 13

Project editor: Janet Illsley
Design: willwebb.co.uk
Printed and bound in Italy by Graphicom

While every effort has been made to ensure the accuracy of the information contained in this book,
in no circumstances can the publisher or the author accept any legal responsibility or liability for
any loss or damage (including damage to property and/or personal injury) arising from any error in
or omission from the information contained in this book, or from the failure of the reader to properly
and accurately follow any instructions contained in the book.

www.bloomsbury.com/rivercottage

www.rivercottage.net

Contents

I love jam and all its jarred and bottled relatives, the extended family we call by the rather austere name 'preserves'. Actually they're not austere at all. They are warm, forward and friendly, offering up both generous feisty flavours and intriguing spicy subtleties to all who embrace them.

Mostly, I love them for being so delicious. But I also cherish and admire them for something else. They epitomise the values at the heart of a well-run, contented kitchen. Firstly they embody and thrive on seasonal abundance. Secondly they are, or should be, intrinsically local, perfectly complementing the grow-your-own (or at least pick-your-own) philosophy. And thirdly, not to be sniffed at in these days of ecological anxiety, they are frugal, thrifty and parsimonious: they waste not, so we want not.

Jams, chutneys and pickles embrace the seasons, but they also, in an elegant and entirely positive manner, defy them. They do so by stretching the bounty of more abundant months into the sparser ones. We shouldn't underestimate this achievement. Over the centuries, wizards and alchemists have used all the power and magic they can muster to try and catch rainbows, spin straw into gold, and even bring the dead back to life. They've failed of course. Yet all the while, humble peasants and ordinary housewives have got on with the simple business of bottling sunshine, so that it may spread a little joy in the leaner seasons ... They call it jam.

More prosaically, I love the way that a couple of hours in the kitchen transforms a gardener's problem into a cook's delight. Come August and September, when it starts raining plums and you are wading through thigh-sized marrows, your conscience would be rightly pricked if you threw such bounty on the compost heap. But when you know how to bottle your own fruit and vegetables, a glut of apples or a pile of pears becomes an exciting opportunity rather than a headache.

Yet I know many keen cooks, even some gardener cooks, who never make preserves. They love eating them, they love receiving them as gifts, they love the *idea* of making them, but something is holding them back. What is it? A fear, perhaps, of the perceived paraphernalia of jam-making, a mild hysteria about the dangers of boiling sugar, a rumbling anxiety about the setting point. I know that such worries are unfounded, delusional even. So what can I do for these poor souls?

Well, I can introduce them to Pam Corbin. I first heard about 'Pam the Jam' when she was running Thursday Cottage Preserves, a small commercial jam company which operated in an almost domestic way, making old-fashioned preserves the old-fashioned way, with real ingredients. When we started planning our Preserving Days at River Cottage, I knew Pam was the person for the job. She shares her passion and wealth of knowledge with enviable clarity and enthusiasm. Many of her sentences end with, 'It's simple, really,' and with Pam to guide you, you really believe it is.

As this book has come together, my admiration for Pam has deepened. She is a great communicator who bestows infectious confidence on her charges. But more than that, she is a woman of decisive palate and impeccable good taste. Throughout the growing year that it took to produce this book, I was the lucky recipient of regular 'jamograms' – little parcels of tasting pots of recipes that she was developing for the book.

From her Early rhubarb jam to Roasted sweet beet relish, Bramley lemon curd to Roasted tomato ketchup, they were invariably exquisite. Your ambitions may be as modest as a few jars of perfect strawberry jam, but under Pam's guidance I'm quite confident that you will soon be dabbling with Blackberry and apple leather, Nasturtium 'capers', Figgy mostardo and Elixir of sage. Just writing their names makes me hungry.

Sadly there wasn't room for all of Pam's fabulous recipes in this book. But it is a tribute to her remarkable gifts that every time we decided to leave one out it felt like a minor tragedy. The upside is that every recipe that's in here is a tried and trusted gem. They met with universal approval from the River Cottage tasting panel – not a formal body, you understand, but a dangerous scrummage of whoever was around when Pam dropped by with a few more jars or bottles.

Pam's approach is not didactic, but encouraging and adventurous. Her message is that, once you've mastered a few basic techniques, there's really no stopping you. In this inspiring book she will show you the ropes and then give you the reins. I'm absolutely sure you will enjoy the ride.

Hugh Fearnley-Whittingstall, Dorset, May 2008

Seasonality

Preserving the bounties of our fruitful summer and autumn

was normal – a way of life – not so many years ago. It was essential to stock up the larder for leaner months, when fresh food was scarce or unavailable and the sealed bottles and jars full of 'summer' would help to allay the monotony of the winter diet. If soft summer currants and berries – and gluts of sweet-smelling tomatoes and trugs of veg – weren't *kept* in some form or another, then there would be no summer produce until the following year. There was no nipping down to the supermarket to buy, in the midst of January, a punnet of strawberries or even a bag of tomatoes.

You don't need to turn the clock back far, just a couple of generations to the 1950s, when to own a home refrigerator or a freezer was considered opulent, and of course fresh foods didn't arrive each day of the week, each week of the year by air and sea from all corners of the globe to flood shop shelves with produce that would otherwise be considered out of season.

The rationing of food during wartime Britain finally finished in July 1954, nine years after the war had ended. The war years had seen the government allocating sugar to the Women's Institute for jam-making so that surplus produce did not go to waste. The extent of food preservation by the WI did not stop at jam-making; these resolute ladies also canned fruit and vegetables for the national food supply. The end to those long years of rationing coincided with an increase in the variety of imported foods readily available throughout the year. Unquestionably, for many, this has meant the structure and meaningful importance of working and living the seasons, along with the necessity to preserve and not waste, have vanished from everyday life.

Following the seasons

Food is never more flavoursome nor as good as when it is fresh and in season, making the riches of a good harvest a just reward for anybody who is prepared to take notice of and be guided by the seasons. For me, there's not much to better a freshly dug new potato cooked up with a sprig of garden mint, and how these earthy roots can be thought of as humble is inexplicable as they are a staple food worldwide. If stored correctly (dark and between 5 and 10°C), their firm and starchy bodies will keep naturally for months without any further action to preserve them.

Or, what could surpass devouring a plateful of freshly picked raspberries? These soft juicy berries, however, will keep for barely a day or two before they begin to deteriorate, so action needs to be speedy to preserve them at their best. Raspberries are a wonderfully useful preserving ingredient, for they can be transformed into blissful jam, bottled, turned into berry cordial or used to make fruity vinegar, all to be put away and enjoyed later in the year.

By the very nature of the variable climate linked with each of the four seasons, much of Britain's home-grown produce is available for limited periods, sometimes just a few swift weeks of the year, when crops of gluttish proportion are available to feast upon fresh, and any surplus will be at its best preserved in some way or another. Ideally, produce to be preserved should be as fresh and local as possible, so every tasty scrap of its character is unmistakably captured. However, there are a few exceptions to the *local* rule, and until we see citrus groves swathing the land, the long-standing tradition of making marmalade to preserve the bitter Seville orange will continue, in addition to the use of tart, acidic lemon in all number of preserving and culinary recipes.

The familiarity of the pattern of the seasons and what each offers is fundamental to understanding how the preserving year is entwined with the growing seasons. The *seasonal performance* is undoubtedly the greatest show on earth: a perennial show in four parts running for 365 days of the year with every month taking a worthy and significant role, where complementary ingredients 'brush shoulders' at their growing time. You'll find elderflowers add muscat perfume to gooseberries, pectin-rich redcurrants combine with low-pectin strawberries, and soft fleshy apples will partner seedy blackberries perfectly at autumn time.

The long slender stalks of rhubarb bridge the beginning and the end of each yearly cycle, starting around the time of the spring equinox, when the sun makes the first of its biannual crossings over the equator and the length of day and night are more or less equal. It is now that the first crinkled, sulphur-yellow rhubarb leaves begin to push their way up from the sleepy earth, unfurling to spread their towering umbrella leaves over silken red-green shoots. From here on, and until the quiescence of sleeping winter, there is usually something budding up and getting ready to yield some form of crop for us to harvest, so a sharp eye needs to be employed to avoid missing any of the seasonal gifts each month offers.

Spring

The spring months of April and May are the wake-up time, heralding the burst of new growth from latent pinky-tinged buds and shoots that rapidly change into blossom or velvety spring-green leaves. The feathery soft green foliage of the native beech begins to spill out from hedgerows in late April and early May, just ahead of the elderflowers who run riot in a showy-off way just about everywhere later in the month. Patches of nettles and wild garlic appear on sheltered banks, the tender young leaves just right to be turned into zesty pesto. Protected pockets of land will allow the first tiny green gooseberries of the season to be picked and, like the long red-green rhubarb stalks, these berries are sharp and tart too, almost as if it is nature's way of arousing our dulled taste buds, stimulating and preparing them for the rush of flavours to come. In preserving terms, these two months are still quite a lazy time, a teaser for the months ahead, but they are by no means idle. Use this time to check out your preserving gear (jars, bottles, lids and things) as well as making sure your stocks of sugar, spices and vinegar are plentiful for when the real season kicks off.

Summer

In June we encounter the summer solstice when the daylight hours are at their maximum and the increasing warmth gives rise to a frenzy of growing in all shapes and colours. We see the start of the soft fruit season with strings of shimmering redcurrants and the early varieties of strawberries and raspberries producing their first sweet berries. Aromatic herbs make themselves known and their heady, sweet-smelling leaves can be used to augment vinegars and oils, and to flavour pesto and relishes. The hedgerow shyly reveals diminutive silver-grey bramble buds, whilst the petals of *Rosa canina* (dog rose) can be gathered to add fragrance to jams, jellies, cordials and spirits. Down in the vegetable garden the first fattening roots of sweet beetroot and the swollen heads of Florence fennel will be beginning to show.

July is the month when the wooden spoon begins to get busy. The early soft fruit berries and currants of June extend to welcome maincrop varieties along with other currant and berry friends; blackcurrants, blueberries, tayberries and loganberries crop plentifully and gooseberries reach sweet maturity to end their productive reign. The silver-grey bramble buds of June break into pink-tinged white flowers, soon to metamorphose into the unmistakable drupelets of indigenous blackberries. Look closely at the elder bush and you'll see a mass of green under-ripe berries, which before long will glisten red-black as they ripen. Hips and haws are like hedgerow chameleons, disguised in their leafy green coats before they first tinge bronze and then blush red for their autumnal show. Cherries, the first of the stone fruits, will be ready, but be quick – they won't last long, and eagle-eyed birds will be waiting to gorge upon them. Greengages and plums are beginning to swell, but it won't be until late in the month or the beginning of August that the early varieties of these orchard fruits will be ready.

August is the true glut month when green beans, courgettes, tomatoes, cucumbers and summer veg invariably oversupply, resulting in a glorious month to preserve as much as possible. The summer-fruiting raspberries are soon replaced by the first flush of blackberries – always the sweetest and juiciest of the year. Watch out for hanging clusters of scarlet rowans, the berries of the mountain ash, for these, combined with a handful of crab apples, will make an outstanding jelly of carnelian colour.

Autumn

In September, you'll find your back step will become a home for refugee fruit, stuffed into bags and left by well-meaning friends who expect you to make all sorts of magnificent jams, jellies and other preserves. Trying to make sure all is safely gathered before the cooler and shorter days of autumn set in, this month might seem a race against time. But don't panic, you'll find marrows, onions, apples, pears and others have developed protective winter coats and, if carefully stored, will keep for a month or two, to use later in the year.

Orchard fruits will now be ripening. Plums, apples and pears yield freely, ahead of the fragrant quince ready at the tail end of the month – watch out though, for too much moisture will make these golden beauties split. For wild food foragers, hedgerows are ablaze with colour, intense with berries and fruits of all kinds; blackberries, rosehips, haws, elders, blue-bloomed sloes, scabby crabs (apples) and clusters of hazelnuts adorn native trees and bushes.

From here on, things really do begin to slow up. Much of the autumn harvest will be past its best. The woodland birds will have feasted well upon the hedgerow spread, although bitter sloes still clinging to thorny branches are for the taking, to imbue fruit liqueurs with their tartness. Apples and pears are still plentiful to turn into Christmas mincemeat or spicy chutney, and onions pickled now will be just right for the festive season. Sweet chestnuts, split from spiky armour, can be found in heaps of fallen leaves, while raspberries, of the autumn kind, stretch berry-picking to this time.

Winter

As the year spins towards the winter solstice, the shorter, darkening days and the lack of sunlight hours allow the earth to rest from growing. The dormancy of the winter begins and only hardy leeks, blue-green brassicas and a few rooty crops survive the cold. But still, within the cycle of the seasonal preserving year, there are two highlights yet to come. The bitter marmalade oranges from Seville arrive in early January, turning this month into a preserving stronghold of the year, when steamy citrus vapours fill our kitchens, and larder shelves are replenished with jars of golden, amber and tawny marmalade to last the year ahead.

Then finally, early rhubarb arrives to carry us through to the next perennial cycle. From late January to early March in darkened sheds and under tall forcing pots, the leaves force upwards to boast the beauty of their slender, translucent pink stalks, heralding the start of another seasonal year.

Seasonal availability

The chart overleaf gives an indication as to when seasonal produce is available. Inevitably though, it can vary by up to 4 weeks depending on how far south or north you live, or if you live in a frost pocket, exposed to cold winds, or a warm, sunny sheltered site. I've not included any indoor-grown crops (with the exception of forced early rhubarb) that rely on indoor heat for their growing cycle.

	JAN	FEB	MAR	APR	MAY
Apples (cooking)	•	•			
Apples (crab)					
Apples (eating)	•	•			
Asparagus					•
Beech leaves					•
Beetroot					
Blackberries					
Blackcurrants					
Blueberries					
Cherries					
Chestnuts					
Chilli peppers					
Cucumbers					
Damsons					
Elderberries					
Elderflowers					•
Fennel					
Figs					
Gooseberries					
Greengages					
Horseradish root					
Hedgerow berries					
Hazelnuts					
Lemons (imported)	•	•	•		
Nasturtium seeds					
Onions					
Pears					
Peppers					
Plums					
Quince					
Raspberries (summer)					
Raspberries (autumn)					
Redcurrants					
Rhubarb (forced)	•	•	•		
Rhubarb (field)				•	•
Rowan berries					
Seville oranges (imported)	•	•			
Runner beans					
Strawberries					•
Tomatoes (outdoor)					

JUNE	JULY	AUG	SEPT	OCT	NOV	DEC
			•	•	•	•
		•	•	•		
		•	•	•	•	•
•						
	•	•	•	•		
	•	•	•	•		
	•	•				
	•	•	•			
•	•	•				
				•	•	
		•	•	•		
		•	•			
		•	•			
		•	•	•		
•						
•	•					
			•			
•	•					
	•	•				
				•	•	
		•	•	•		
			•	•	•	
					•	•
	•	•	•			
	•	•	•	•		
			•	•	•	
			•	•		
	•	•	•			
			•	•	•	
	•	•	•			
			•		•	
	•	•				
•	•					
		•	•			
	•	•	•			
•	•	•	•			
	•	•	•			

Fruit-growing regions in Britain

With an agreeable, temperate climate and a patchwork of differing soils, Britain bestows an abundance of fruit from all corners of the land. From the rich loamy lowland of the eastern counties to the verdant pastures of the West Country, the good earth not only gives crops the food and energy needed to sustain growth, but it also instils character in the fruit it bears. In turn, regions become strongly associated with their produce. Somerset is indelibly linked with cider apples, for example, while the fruit orchards of Kent give it the title 'garden of England'.

Some of these areas are mere pockets of land covering as little as a few hectares, like the rambling orchards along the river Fal in Cornwall, where the tart 'Kea' plum survives the salt-laden southwesterlies. Other larger regions embrace neighbouring counties, forming well-known commercial growing areas. The drier, colder eastern terrain, for example, is home to many British-grown strawberries, with names such as 'Early Cambridge', 'Cambridge Favourite' and 'Cambridge Vigour' sealing their origins. Grown too in this region is the unique and intensely flavoured darling 'Little Scarlet' strawberry, used for over a century by Essex jam-makers Wilkin & Sons. As many as seventy of these tiny sweet strawberries are packed into a jar of their highly acclaimed jam.

In western terrains you will find a network of ancient and established orchards crisscrossing and bordering pasture land. This large area splits down into smaller regions, which offer different varieties that assume native rights to the soil and climate they inhabit. Bittersweet, sharp and sweet, juicy apples for cider-making predominate the Devonshire and Somerset orchards, whereas the Vale of Evesham in southern Worcestershire is famed for the luscious plums, dessert apples and pears it bears. Here, in the wetter, warmer West, apples and pears put on their natural waxy waterproof coats to protect their fleshy fruit from the southwesterly precipitations.

Surprisingly, perhaps, despite the obvious contrast in climate, good commercial crops of soft berries and currants grow in both the North and South of the country. One noticeable difference is that 'high bush' members of the *Vaccinium* or blueberry family are cultivated in the safe and sheltered South, whereas 'low bush' relatives are those that are found growing wild on heath and moorland in the rather more vigorous climes of northern England and Scotland.

The rich fertile 'middling lands' sustain a fusion and miscellany of fruit-growing – from *ribes* to rhubarb and much in between. Good crops of blackcurrants flourish in the West Midlands, while the village of Timperley in Cheshire has long been famed for its field rhubarb 'Timperley Early' – a cultivar whose name and excellence dominates the rhubarb world. Gooseberries are another popular traditional crop in this part of the country.

The nineteenth century saw the start-up of gooseberry shows in the North and Midlands counties of Cheshire, Lancashire, Yorkshire, Derbyshire, Staffordshire and Nottinghamshire. Gooseberry enthusiasts grew (and still do in a handful of villages) outsize berries in the hope of winning the premier prize for the heaviest berry of the show. 'Ringer', 'London', 'Lancashire Lad', 'Lady Leicester' and 'Wonderful' are but a few of these weighty wonders. The berries were weighed by pennyweights (equivalent to 1.555g) and the heaviest 'London' ever recorded weighed in at just over 37dwt (58g) in 1852 – quite a monster to meet in a pie! Mind you, no show went without a tipple or two ...

Gooseberry growers' anthem

Come all you jovial gardeners and listen unto me
Whilst I relate the different sorts of winning Gooseberries
This famous Institution was founded long ago
That men might meet and drink and have a Gooseberry Show ...

Northwards, to the eastern edge of the Pennines, a district has become known as the 'Yorkshire Triangle'. Here, the heavy clay soil and the cold climate provide the right conditions for forcing rhubarb in darkened sheds during the short days of January and February; the frost is needed to kick-start the growth of the sweet, succulent soft shoots of this indoor-grown crop. The availability of coal from nearby mines was used to heat the forcing sheds until the mid 1980s but the miners' strike of 1984–5 obliged growers such as Oldroyd's to use kerosene and propane to heat the sheds, as they still do today.

To the west of the high Pennines in one of the wettest regions of Britain, the small Westmorland damson thrives in the hedgerows of the Lyth and Winster valleys. Related to the 'Shropshire' plum, it has grown here for three centuries or more. The flavour of this damson is unique and the skins provide a deep-purple dye for the northern woollen industry.

Over the border in Scotland, the cool conditions of the eastern and central counties of Perthshire, Angus and Fife provide excellent growing conditions for raspberries, strawberries and blackcurrants with such names as 'Ben Nevis', 'Ben Hope' 'Glen Moy' and 'Glen Ample' confirming their ancestral roots, whilst Tayside is the natural home to the red-black tayberry.

The chart overleaf gives an indication of principal growing areas in Britain, but by no means are these particular growing areas dedicated to growing *only* these fruits nor do the fruits listed *only* grow in them. Most regions, save for the highlands and moorlands, will grow a mixture of produce, and even here the odd elder or blackberry will flourish.

REGION	PRINCIPAL CROPS	SPECIALITIES
South-west – Cornwall, Devon, Dorset, Somerset	Cider apples Eating apples Blackcurrants Cherries Strawberries	'Dittisham Black' plum (Devon) 'Kea' plum (Cornwall)
Southern England	Cherries Blackcurrants Strawberries	Blueberries (south-east Dorset)
South-east England – Kent, Surrey, Sussex	Eating and cooking apples Blackcurrants Cherries Gooseberries Pears Plums Strawberries	Cobnuts (Kent)
Eastern counties – Essex, Cambridgeshire, Suffolk, Norfolk, Lincolnshire	Bramley apples Cherries Gooseberries Pears Strawberries	'Cambridge Gage' 'Worcester Pearmain' apple
West Midlands/ Welsh Border	Blackcurrants Damsons Eating apples Greengages Plums Pears	Perry pear 'Pershore' plum
North Midlands	Damsons Field rhubarb	
Northern England	Damsons Forced rhubarb	
Eastern and Central Scotland	Blackcurrants Strawberries Raspberries	Tayberries
National – rampant and everywhere	Blackberries Elderflowers/berries Hedgerow fruits and berries Apples	

The Rules

Preserving evokes

Preserving evokes deep-rooted, almost primeval feelings of self-sufficiency and survival, of gatherer and hunter, for this is how our ancestors stayed alive. These days this all sounds more than a little extreme, but unquestionably a home with a good store of home-made preserves will generate a feeling of warmth and confidence.

I admit that at times I can get quite carried away thinking of how I can fill shapely jam jars, of the glistening grains of sugar, the neroli-like perfume of Seville oranges ... But I've also found that it pays to be aware of a small amount of cold, hard science, and to be familiar with some basic but important practical techniques. Once you understand why food goes off, and how it can be prevented from doing so, your jam-, jelly- and chutney-making can reach new levels of success. Don't worry, you don't need a chemistry degree ...

The simple fact is that any fresh food, unless it is treated in some way, will inevitably decay and become unsuitable for consumption. There are four meddlesome elements that cause spoilage in foods – enzymes, bacteria, moulds/fungi and yeasts – but, if the cook intervenes to prevent or arrest their progress, most foods can be safely kept for extended periods of time.

The four spoilers

Micro-organisms are generally viewed as undesirable and if present in sufficient numbers they make food a health hazard. In certain conditions, all micro-organisms will flourish and increase. Some non-harmful micro-organisms are deliberately brought into play in food production, of course – mould in blue cheeses, and yeasts in beer- and bread-making, for example – but it is the harmful micro-organisms that concern us in preserve-making.

Good food hygiene is the first step in stopping the spoilers. It is essential that all food be handled with care, and all utensils, equipment and work surfaces be spotlessly clean, so as few micro-organisms as possible are present to start with.

The use of high temperatures is the second way to defeat the tricky foursome – hence cooking being an integral part of many preserving processes. They may thrive in warmth, but they cannot take real heat.

High concentrations of sugar, acid, alcohol or salt also kill these undesirables, or at the very least make it hard for them to flourish, and nearly all the preserving techniques in this book rely on large quantities of these ingredients to create conditions hostile to enzymes and micro-organisms.

The final line of attack involves excluding the air which these spoilers need to thrive. This is why well-sealed jars and bottles are essential, and why oil is another important preserving medium.

Enzymes

These are not actually organisms, but proteins found in all living things, animal or vegetable, and they perform a huge variety of roles. From a culinary point of view, it's important to know that enzymes remain active long after food has been harvested, and they function as catalysts for change, triggering and speeding up chemical processes. Enzymes trigger deterioration, for instance, by sparking off changes in tissue that in turn provide a fertile environment for the growth of micro-organisms. The discolouring of cut or damaged fruit or vegetables is also caused by enzyme action. However, if the exposed surface comes into contact with an acid or alkali, the discoloration will slow down. This is why prepared produce is often rubbed with lemon juice or plunged into lightly salted water.

Enzymes increase their activity at temperatures between 29 and 50°C and will begin to be destroyed at temperatures above 60°C. Their action is also halted at temperatures below freezing point but will increase again when warmth returns.

Bacteria

So small that they are only visible under a microscope, these are the most ancient and widespread form of life on earth. Bacteria increase rapidly at temperatures between 20 and 40°C. They become dormant in the freezer, and are destroyed at or near 100°C – the boiling point of water. Bacterial spoilage of food is sometimes difficult to detect, and although most bacteria are harmless – some even useful – some cause food to rot and become foul-smelling, and their toxins are harmful to health. It is therefore vital not to take any shortcuts with preserving procedures, and to follow all instructions carefully to avoid any form of bacterial contamination.

Moulds and fungi

The spores of these micro-organisms are present in the air around us and will take root in almost any food. Initially they produce fine threads, then the characteristic grey-green, cotton-wool-like bloom. Moulds and fungi are dormant at 0°C, thrive at temperatures between 10 and 38°C, and their spoiling activities decrease from 60 to 88°C, which is why cooking is an efficient way to get rid of them. A bit of mould on the top of an open jar of jam should not be scooped off and ignored; as they grow, some moulds produce mycotoxins that can be harmful if eaten.

Yeasts

The yeasts found in foods are generally not harmful to health but can cause spoilage. Most species are quickly destroyed at 60°C and above, and are inactivated by cold. Some grow in food containing as much as 60 per cent sugar and badly covered or half-used jars of jam stored in a warm kitchen are prime sites for yeasts to begin to ferment; also gases are produced, which may cause the preserve to 'blow' in the jar.

Potting, packing and sealing

Proper potting and sealing is one of the main pillars of good preserve-making. If done incorrectly, it can ruin a batch of otherwise perfect preserves. These days, some form of glass vessel with a secure seal is generally used. To reduce the risk of bacterial contamination, it is important to sterilise the container and fully fill or 'jam-pack' it with your preserve.

Sterilising jars

Any micro-organism lurking in the container you put your preserve into has the potential to grow and contaminate, which is why it is essential to use sterile jars. There are three simple ways to sterilise jars: you can immerse them in a pan of water and bring to the boil; or wash them in very hot, soapy water, rinse thoroughly, then dry them in a very low oven; alternatively, you can simply put them through a hot dishwasher cycle.

Whichever method you choose, only clean the jars shortly before they are to be used and make sure they are dry. This minimises time in which the jars might pick up new bacteria. Also, all hot preserves should be poured into warm jars (this helps to prevent the temperature dropping before the seal is applied), so you might as well use them before they have cooled down from the drying process.

Recycling jars and bottles

I like to reuse and recycle jars and bottles wherever possible. As well as keeping costs down, it gives me a wide variety of shapes and sizes to choose from. However, recycled jars should always be cleaned both inside and outside, then very carefully examined to make sure they are not damaged in any way. Cracks or chips are ideal breeding grounds for bacteria and can also shed tiny splinters of glass that could cause injury if swallowed.

Old labels on recycled jars should be fully removed. I find the best way of attacking this job is to fully immerse the jars in a pan of cold water, bring to simmering point and simmer for 10 minutes. I then let the jars cool and, when cool enough to handle, rub the label off with the blunt side of a knife. Tamper-seals and labels on lids can be removed in the same way.

If you do want to buy jars, they are available from specialist shops (see the directory, p.210) and are generally sold in certain sizes that comply with the requirements for commercially produced preserves. The sizes are always given as a volume rather than a weight, and the chart overleaf gives the equivalent approximate weight and volume capacities. However, if you are using an assortment of recycled jars, you might find it easier to measure their capacity in volume (just fill them with water then tip into a measuring jug).

Jar sizes

Before you start making a preserve, you should check the recipe to see how many jars you will need so you can have them ready.

METRIC WEIGHT	IMPERIAL WEIGHT	VOLUME
113g	4oz	100ml
225g	8oz	195ml
340g	12oz	290ml
454g	1lb	380ml
680g	1½lb	570ml
900g	2lb	760ml

Thankfully, almost all jars share just two or three lid sizes, so lids can often be mixed and matched between various jars and bottles.

Sealing jars

Having potted your preserve, the next vital thing is to seal it as quickly as possible to prevent entry of oxygen and airborne micro-organisms. For hot sweet preserves, chutneys and relishes there are two principal ways in which this can be done – with a cellophane cover or a twist-on lid. Pickles and vinegar preserves should always be sealed with vinegar-proof twist-on lids.

I like to seal fruit cheeses by pouring melted 'food grade' paraffin wax over the surface, giving a really traditional finish to the filled pots. The easiest way to melt the wax is to place it in a heatproof bowl (I keep one especially for this) and stand it in a pan of gently simmering water until the wax is liquid.

Cellophane covers Place a waxed disc, wax side down, on the hot surface of the preserve, then cover the jar with a cellophane disc, securing it tightly with an elastic band. This is best done when the jar is still hot. Cellophane covers can also be applied when the jars are completely cold but should never be put on when the jar is tepid as this can cause mould growth.

Before putting on the cellophane, make sure the rim of the jar is clean. With a drop of water, moisten one side of the cover to make it stretch, then position with the damp side uppermost. Secure with a rubber band. As the cellophane dries, it will contract to give a tight lid. Packs of waxed discs, cellophane covers, elastic bands and labels are available in supermarkets and kitchen shops, and from mail order suppliers (see the directory, p.210).

Twist-on lids The metal twist-on/off lids that come with most jars are very easy to use and create a good tight seal. Generally, these days, most lids have a plasticised lining that is 'food law approved' and suitable for use with both sugar- and vinegar-based preserves. Avoid the use of unlined metal lids with vinegar preserves because they will corrode and spoil the preserve. For the best possible results, I recommend always using new lids, even with recycled jars. Previously used lids are still an option but you must make sure they are not damaged in any way and they should be sterilised by boiling in a pan of water for 10 minutes before use.

Bottles

I stash away recycled bottles of various shapes and sizes to use when making cordials, fruit liqueurs, flavoured vinegars and oils. Vinegar bottles with screw-top lids are excellent for flavoured vinegars, cordials and squashes, while small, interesting-shaped spirit bottles are jolly useful for fruit liqueurs and make attractive gifts.

A good range of bottles can be purchased from specialist suppliers (see the directory, p.210), including old-fashioned preserving bottles with a swing-top lid fastening. I particularly like using these nice-looking bottles: made from toughened glass, they are easy to use, the lid is attached and they can be used time and time again. All bottles, lids and corks should be sterilised by boiling for 10 minutes in a pan of water before use.

Filling and sealing

Careful potting and sealing at the correct temperature for the particular preserve is important for the keeping quality.

TYPE OF PRESERVE	TEMPERATURE	NOTES
Jams, jellies, fruit butters and cheeses, marmalades	Hot-fill (preserve should be above 85–90°C) warm, dry jars, to within 3mm of the rim	Allow whole fruit jams and chunky marmalades to stand for 10–15 minutes after cooking, before putting into jars
Fruit curds	Fill warm jars as soon as the curd is cooked	For entry into local horticultural shows, fruit curds must be covered with wax disc and cellophane seal
Chutneys, relishes, sauces and ketchups	Hot-fill warm, dry jars	Remove air pockets by sharply tapping the jars. Use vinegar-proof lids. Some sauces may need to be sterilised in a water bath (see p.164)
Pickles and sweet pickles	Hot or cold-fill clean, dry jars to within 5mm of the rim	Use vinegar-proof lids. Remove air pockets by sharply tapping the jars
Fruit syrups	Hot-fill clean bottles and seal immediately	To extend shelf life, sterilise in a water bath or oven (see pp.164–6)
Bottled fruits	It is essential to follow individual recipes precisely	See Bottled Fruits (pp.158–85)
Oil and alcohol-based preserves	Cold-fill. Make sure ingredients are totally immersed before sealing	Remove air pockets by sharply tapping jars. Seal with a twist-on lid

Labelling

Use self-adhesive labels with plenty of space to record what the preserve is and when it was made. Plain labels can be used but there are lots of attractive labels on the market designed especially for preserve-making. If you're a dab hand on the computer, you can even design your own. Don't try to stick a label to a hot jar – the glue will melt and it will fall off. Wait until jars are cold before labelling.

Safe keeping

A preserve with a good seal should last a long time, although the texture and colour may well deteriorate. None the less, I'd be the first to admit that a murky jar of some old concoction, discovered during a larder clear-out, will have little appeal – and there is always an underlying concern that it might have gone off. The following are guidelines for safe keeping and pleasant eating. (Chutneys, pickles and marmalades, by the way, improve with a maturing period so shouldn't be eaten straight away.)

Once opened, look after your preserves. Replace lids securely and keep the preserve in a cool place because, once the seal on a jar or bottle is broken, the contents are vulnerable and can be re-contaminated by micro-organisms.

PRESERVE	IDEAL SHELF LIFE
Fruit curds	Use within 4 weeks. Store in the fridge once opened
Vegetables in oil	Use within 4 months. Refrigerate one opened and use within 6 weeks
Pesto	Store in the fridge and use within 4 weeks
Fruit butters	Use within 9 months and refrigerate once opened
Jams and jellies	Use within 1 year
Fruit cheeses	Use within 1 year and refrigerate once opened
Mincemeat	Use within 1 year
Relishes	Use within 1 year. Store in the fridge once opened
Sauces	Use within 1 year
Chutneys and pickles	Store for 4–10 weeks before using. Use within 1–2 years
Marmalades	Use within 2 years
Alcohol preserves	Use within 3 years

In a cool, dry, dark place These conditions apply to the storage of all preserves. Few houses these days have good old-fashioned larders or cellars so you may find the best place to keep your preserves is in the garage or shed.

Key preserving ingredients

Most of the ingredients needed for preserving are in general use in a busy kitchen. It is, however, worth considering their different characteristics.

Sugar

A concentration of over 60 per cent sugar in a preserve creates an environment that is hostile to micro-organisms. Sugar can also be combined with vinegar in sweet-and-sour preserves such as chutneys and sauces. The sugar you use not only affects the cooking process but also influences the final flavour of your preserves:

Granulated sugar Available in pure white or golden, unrefined varieties, this is a good basic, inexpensive sugar that will work well in almost any of the recipes in this book. It has medium-coarse grains so takes a little longer to dissolve than fine-grained caster sugar but is less likely to stick to the bottom of the pan and burn. Granulated sugar is produced in Britain, from sugar beet (Silver Spoon is one brand), but an intensive refining process is involved. If you'd prefer an unrefined sugar, which will retain its natural golden colour and delicate caramel flavour, choose an imported one, derived from sugar cane. Billingtons produce an unrefined, organic, golden granulated, and also a fair trade variety. I use both unrefined and refined granulated sugar. Golden, unrefined sugar is ideal for marmalades, and with strong-flavoured fruits such as blackcurrants, but I prefer a refined white sugar for more delicate fruits and berries, for jellies and curds, and for flavoured liqueurs.

Large-grain preserving sugar This is more costly than granulated sugars. It's by no means essential for good preserves but the big, chunky crystals dissolve slowly, need less stirring and are less likely to stick to the bottom of the pan. They also produce less froth or scum. Preserving sugar does not generally contain added pectin.

Jam sugar This usually signifies a sugar with added pectin – and sometimes citric acid too. It's ideal for use with low-pectin fruits such as rhubarb and strawberries and will ensure a quick and easy set. However, don't use it with pectin-rich fruits like gooseberries, plums and Seville oranges – the set will be more like wallpaper paste.

Brown sugar Using unrefined demerara or muscovado sugar in a jam or chutney – either wholly, or in combination with a lighter sugar – changes the colour and taste. These dark sugars are not highly processed and are full

of natural molasses flavour. They can overpower delicate ingredients but are wonderful when used with citrus fruit in marmalades or with vinegar and spices in savoury chutneys and pickles.

Honey This can be used to add another layer of flavour to a preserve, although it cannot entirely replace the sugar as it burns very easily. Supplement 10–15 per cent of the total sugar in a recipe with honey and add it when the sugar has dissolved.

Vinegar

Vinegar has been used for centuries to preserve everything from onions to eggs, and foods preserved in this medium are generally referred to as being 'pickled'. The word 'vinegar' comes from the medieval French *vin-aigre,* meaning 'sour wine'. It is produced by a double fermentation of some form of fruit or grain. The first fermentation is brought about by yeasts turning sugar into alcohol, as in the production of wine, beer and cider. The second fermentation involves bacteria turning the alcohol to acetic acid, thereby creating vinegar.

In order to preserve successfully, the acetic acid content of vinegar must be at least 5 per cent – check the label. This level of acidity creates an environment where few micro-organisms can survive. The harsh flavour of vinegar can be mitigated by the addition of sugar and/or spices, while the choice of vinegar itself will also have a considerable effect on the final taste of your pickles:

Malt vinegar Produced from fermented barley, malt vinegar is inexpensive and has been the backbone of traditional pickling for many years. It has a very strong taste which some people love, but I often find it a bit too aggressive. Nevertheless, in a really hearty, well-spiced chutney or pickle, it can give precisely the right robust bass note of flavour and is a stalwart favourite for pickled onions. The colour in dark malt vinegars comes from the addition of caramel – pure, distilled malt vinegar is colourless.

Wine vinegars Derived from grapes, red and white wine vinegars are more expensive than malt but have a finer, more delicate flavour. I like to use them for pickling ingredients such as nasturtium pods, where I don't want the pods' fiery bite swamped by vinegar.

Cider vinegar This is sweeter and fruitier than wine vinegar and my choice for seasonal chutneys, pickles and relishes. Aspall's (see the directory, p.210) sells an excellent range of home-produced cider vinegars and, if you live in cider apple country, you may well find some excellent local varieties.

Salt

High concentrations of salt are of course inimical to yeast, bacteria and moulds, which is why this ingredient is so important in many preserving methods. Salt is also crucial for enhancing flavour. In addition, it is often used in the preparation of foods prior to pickling, where it draws out excess water, which would otherwise dilute and spoil the preserve (see Pickles, Chutneys & Relishes, p.92).

Sea salt This is produced by evaporating sea water. You can buy unrefined, natural flaky types, such as Maldon or Halen Môn, which are lovely sweet-tasting ingredients. They are also much more expensive than other salts so, while you might be happy to use them for seasoning, you may think it rather extravagant to use them in large quantities for dry-salting or pickling. A relatively inexpensive fine-grained sea salt, available from health food stores or supermarkets, is what I use most often in preserving. It's certainly the most suitable type for dry-salting vegetables for pickling, as it will coat them well. However, like many fine-grained, free-flowing salts, some fine sea salts contain an anti-caking agent, so do check labels before you buy.

Rock salt Generally the cheaper alternative to sea salt, this is mined from underground mineral deposits. It may also be sold as kitchen salt or table salt. Some is highly processed, purified and treated and tastes correspondingly harsh. I don't use salts like this in preserving as they can affect the final quality of the preserve. However, coarse, additive-free rock salts, such as Tidman's, are available, and make a good alternative to sea salt.

Alcohol

This is a very useful preserving medium but, to function effectively, it must be in the form of a spirit that is at least 40 per cent alcohol (80 per cent proof). Gin, vodka, rum, brandy and whisky are all suitable. Gin is a tried-and-tested favourite with fruits such as sloes and damsons, while stoned cherries will make a splendid liqueur when steeped in brandy. Colourless eau de vie (brandy or flavourless alcohol that has not been aged) is an ideal base for more delicate or subtle ingredients. Wines, fortified wines and cider can be used for preserving but need to be combined with other preservative ingredients such as sugar, or with sterilising methods such as bottling.

Oil

An effective means of sealing out oxygen, oil is a useful and potentially delicious part of many savoury preserves. The oil will be an integral part of the finished preserve and, as it will have taken on flavour from the preserved food, you might want to use it to enhance other dishes. So I'd advise always using the best you can afford.

Olive oil This is extracted by grinding olives to a paste and then pressing with large millstones. 'Extra virgin' refers to olive oil with very low acidity, which is completely unrefined and taken from the first pressing of the olives. It's considered to be the very best type. However, it is expensive, and often powerfully flavoured, and I rarely use it in preserves. 'Virgin' olive oil has a little more acidity, but is also unrefined and will have a good flavour. It is much more affordable, and my choice for most oil-based preserves. Anything labelled 'pure' olive oil, or just 'olive oil' will be a blend of refined and unrefined oils. Less exciting, they are still perfectly acceptable to use.

Sunflower oil Light in colour, almost flavourless, and much less expensive than olive oil, a good-quality sunflower oil is useful when you don't want the taste of the oil to intrude on the preserve. It can also be blended with other, more robustly flavoured oils (see below).

Rapeseed oil Golden in colour and nutty in flavour, this is extracted from the tiny, jet-black seeds of *Brassica napus*, a member of the mustard family, and is often home-produced. It contains less saturated fat than any other oil, is high in omega 3 and is a good source of vitamin E. I like to use it for flavoured oils.

Hemp oil Cold-pressed hemp oil is vivid green in colour and has a very strong nutty flavour. Again, it can be grown and processed in this country. Alone, it would be overpowering for many ingredients, but 10–15 per cent blended with sunflower oil creates a well-flavoured oil.

Equipment for preserving

Kitting yourself out for preserving will not entail a second mortgage. You probably already have most of the equipment you need in your kitchen. Here is a very quick run-through of essentials and useful items:

Preserving pan Sometimes called a maslin pan, this is almost an essential item – but a large, wide, heavy-bottomed stock pot could stand in. Preserving pans do have the advantages of sloping sides which maximise evaporation, a pouring lip and a strong carrying handle. Go for a robust stainless-steel one of approximately 9-litre capacity. This should be large enough for most jamming and chutney sessions. Your pan must be deep enough to contain the rapid rise in liquid that occurs when jam comes to a full rolling boil. It

is useful to buy one with a calibrated volume measure on the inside of the pan which allows you to see by how much your ingredients have reduced.

Wooden spoons These need to be big and long-handled. If possible, keep one especially for jam and one for chutney-making (they will become impregnated with fruity and vinegary juices respectively).

Preserving or sugar thermometer This is not expensive and will help you to check that your preserves have reached the right temperature for setting point, as well as giving you an accurate guide to temperature when bottling.

Slotted spoon For skimming scum or fishing out fruit stones.

Sieves A couple of heatproof nylon sieves are useful for puréeing fruit – the acid from which can react with a metal sieve.

Paper coffee filters For straining small quantities of fruit vinegar or liqueur.

Mouli or food mill Great labour-saving tool for puréeing fruits and removing skins and pips simultaneously. Useful when making fruit butters and cheeses.

Jelly bag, or muslin, and stand These are essential for straining the juice from cooked fruit when making jellies. Purpose-made jelly bags and stands are available from specialist shops (see the directory, p.210). Or you can improvise, using an upturned stool with a double thickness of muslin tied to each leg to form a bag. Jelly bags and muslin can be re-used, even though they become stained by fruit dyes. Before use (even when new) they should be scalded by placing in a pan of water and bringing to the boil.

Spice infuser Not essential, but an alternative to tying spices in muslin for spicing vinegars and chutneys.

Measuring jugs and spoons One or two calibrated, heat-resistant measuring jugs are indispensable for measuring ingredients and pouring preserves into jars. A set of measuring spoons is also very useful for spices and seasonings.

Funnel A wide-necked pouring funnel can prevent spillages when filling jars but is not essential – a steady hand and a good pouring jug is often easier.

Accurate kitchen scales Very important for preserving success.

Jams & Jellies

This is the sweetest chapter in the book, where you

will meet what I call the 'sugar set'. In other words, recipes that rely purely on a high concentration of sugar to keep spoiling at bay. Sugar-based recipes form a broad and extensive branch of the preserving tree, and they are also the most familiar and perhaps widely used type of preserve. Here you will find out just how essential sugar is as a preserving ingredient and how, by means of various preserving techniques, it can be used to transform a host of fresh produce into goodies that can be safely stored away for the future.

The different types of sugar-based preserve that I make at home are as follows:

Jams Without doubt, jams are the most familiar of all the sweet preserves. They are simply mixtures of lightly softened fruit and sugar, boiled together until they gel into a mass.

Marmalades Although originally referring to a type of quince jam (*marmelo* being the Portuguese word for quince), the term 'marmalade' is now universally understood to mean a bittersweet preserve made from citrus fruit. Marmalades are made in a similar way to jams but the hard citrus peel needs long, slow cooking to soften it before sugar is added.

Conserves Made with whole fruit that has been steeped in sugar before cooking to draw out the juices, a conserve is similar to a jam but often has a slightly softer set. Commercially, the word conserve is often used to describe a posh jam with a high fruit content.

Fruit spreads and fridge jams These are relatively low in sugar and usually made with added pectin to help them set. In general, they still have a softer, looser set than traditional jams. Providing they are sealed when still over 90°C, they will keep for 9–12 months. However, once opened, they must be kept in the fridge as they do not contain sufficient sugar to prevent them spoiling at cool larder temperature.

Jellies Clear, translucent and smooth (no fruity bits), fruit jellies are the jewels of the store cupboard. They are made by boiling strained fruit juice with sugar. They are best made with fruits high in both pectin and acid, such as apples, crab apples, gooseberries and redcurrants – either on their own or in combination with other, lower-pectin fruits (see the pectin/acid content chart on p.48). The basic fruit juice and sugar mixture can also be used as a base for herb or flower jellies.

Fruit butters So called because they spread as 'soft as butter', these are made by boiling cooked, sieved fruit pulp with sugar. They are lower in sugar than traditional jams and will not keep as well. For this reason, they are best potted in smallish jars, which can be consumed in a relatively short time and stored in the fridge once opened.

Fruit cheeses These dense, solid preserves are similar to fruit butters in that they are made by boiling sieved fruit pulp with sugar. However, they are cooked for longer and taste richer and fruitier. You could make a cheese with almost any fruit but, because of the large quantity required, recipes usually favour prolific orchard, stone and hedgerow fruits such as apples, quince, damsons or crab apples. Fruit cheeses are normally packed in straight-sided jars or moulds so the preserve can be turned out whole and sliced.

Fruit curds These are not true preserves, being very low in sugar, but creamy mixtures of butter, eggs, sugar and an acidic fruit pulp or juice. To prevent the eggs curdling, they are cooked very gently in a double boiler or in a basin over a pan of boiling water. Curds are best eaten within 3–4 weeks, so they are usually made in fairly small quantities.

Mincemeats Again, these are not true sugar preserves, as alcohol plays its part in the process too. Mincemeats are mixtures of dried fruit, apples, spices, citrus zest, sugar, suet (sometimes) and alcohol. They are traditionally made in the autumn when the new season's apples are crisp and juicy, then kept for a couple of months to mellow and mature in time to make mince pies for Christmas.

Fruit leathers These rely on drying, as well as sugar, to preserve the fruit. A lightly sweetened purée is slowly dried in a low oven (or, in suitable climates, under the sun), producing a thin, pliable sheet. Fruit leathers store well for several months.

Candied fruits This is a generic term for fruits preserved by being steeped in sugar for a period of time. The sugar penetrates the fruit flesh, replacing some of the natural juices. Different types include glacé fruits, which are coated with a clear sugar syrup, and crystallised fruits, which are rolled in grains of sugar.

The essential foursome

In jam-, jelly- and marmalade-making, four ingredients are necessary to produce the magic result known as 'a set' – i.e. the right wobbling, spreadable consistency. These are fruit, pectin, acid and sugar. Getting to know them will help to ensure success.

Fruit

All fruit for preserve-making should be dry, as fresh as possible and slightly under-ripe. Over-ripe, wet fruit contains less pectin and acid and makes a poor-quality preserve. If you find yourself snowed under with produce during a particularly good cropping season, remember that most fruits, including Seville oranges, can be frozen and used later in the year quite successfully. Bear in mind that the pectin content reduces a little with freezing so sometimes extra pectin may need to be added.

With the exception of the citrus family, I have used only native British fruits in the recipes for this chapter. There are, of course, a whole host of imported exotics at our disposal these days, but buying these in the quantities required for jam-making can be expensive. In any case, with the abundance of home-grown fruits available to us, it's hardly necessary.

Pectin

This is a natural substance found in all fruit (and some vegetables) in varying quantities (see the fruit pectin/acid content chart overleaf). When combined with acid and sugar, it takes on a gum-like consistency – which is why it's essential in achieving a good set. Concentrated in cores, pith, skins and pips, it is released from the cell walls as the fruit is cooked. Pectin levels are at their highest in slightly under-ripe fruit and will decrease as the fruit ripens, or if it is frozen.

Fruit with lots of pectin will produce a jam or jelly that sets easily, while those containing lower amounts may well need a bit of help. This can come from other high-pectin fruits added to the mix (as with blackberry and apple jelly, for instance). Alternatively, extra pectin can be added in the form of a pectin stock (see right), or commercially produced liquid or powdered pectin (usually extracted from apples or citrus fruit). A third option is to use jam sugar with added pectin (see p.35). This is very handy for quick and easy jam-making and, provided the manufacturer's instructions are followed, will guarantee a set with low-pectin fruits such as sweet cherries, rhubarb and strawberries.

> How to test for pectin If you follow the chart overleaf, you shouldn't need to test for pectin. However, if you're using a fruit not covered here, there is a simple way to check the pectin levels. Add 1 tsp (5ml) of the cooked fruit juice to 1 tbsp (15ml) methylated spirits (or gin or whisky, as these work

too). Shake gently and leave for a minute or two. Juice from a pectin-rich fruit will form a firm clot. If the juice forms several small clots, this indicates a medium pectin content. Juice that remains fairly liquid signifies a low pectin level.

Home-made pectin stock A pectin-rich 'stock' is easily made from certain fruits. The procedure is much the same as the early stages of jelly-making:

Combine 1kg redcurrants, gooseberries or roughly chopped (but not peeled or cored) sour cooking apples with 600ml water. Bring to a simmer and cook gently for 45 minutes to 1 hour, or until the fruit is soft. Strain through a jelly bag (see p.41). The resulting pectin stock will keep for up to 4 weeks in the fridge. To keep it longer, either freeze it (but allow for a reduction in strength when using) or sterilise it.

To sterilise, bring the juice to the boil, pour into hot, sterilised preserving jars and seal immediately. Immerse the jars in a pan of hot water with a folded tea towel on the bottom. Heat the water until boiling, then boil for 5 minutes. Remove the jars carefully and store in a cool, dry place.

To use the stock, stir 150–300ml of it into every 1kg of low-pectin, softened fruit before sugar is added.

FRUIT	PECTIN	ACID
Apples (cooking)	HIGH	HIGH
Apples (crab)	HIGH	HIGH
Apples (dessert)	MEDIUM	LOW
Apricots	MEDIUM	LOW
Blackberries (early)	MEDIUM	LOW
Blackberries (late)	LOW	LOW
Blueberries	MEDIUM	HIGH
Citrus fruit	HIGH	HIGH
Cherries (sour)	MEDIUM	HIGH
Cherries (sweet)	LOW	LOW
Currants (red, black and white)	HIGH	HIGH
Damsons	HIGH	HIGH
Elderberries	LOW	LOW
Figs	LOW	LOW
Gooseberries	HIGH	HIGH
Greengages	MEDIUM	MEDIUM
Japonicas	HIGH	HIGH
Loganberries	MEDIUM	HIGH
Medlars	LOW	LOW
Mulberries	MEDIUM	HIGH
Peaches	LOW	LOW
Pears	LOW	LOW
Plums (sweet)	MEDIUM	MEDIUM
Plums (sour)	HIGH	HIGH
Quince	HIGH	LOW
Raspberries (ripe)	MEDIUM	MEDIUM
Raspberries (unripe)	MEDIUM	LOW
Rhubarb	LOW	LOW
Rowan berries	MEDIUM-LOW	HIGH
Sloes	MEDIUM	HIGH
Strawberries	LOW	LOW

Acid

This is naturally found in fruit and is essential for clear, bright, well-set preserves. It draws pectin out of the fruit, enabling setting point to be reached quickly without lengthy cooking, which would darken the jam. Acid also helps prevent crystallisation of the sugar. Levels of acid vary in different fruits (see chart, left) and are lower in over-ripe fruit. Lemon, gooseberry or redcurrant juice is sometimes added to low-acid fruit jams. It should be added before the fruit is cooked, so it can get to work on drawing out the pectin. If you're making jam with a low-acid fruit, such as strawberries or rhubarb, add 30ml lemon juice, or 150ml redcurrant, gooseberry or apple juice, per 1kg of fruit.

Sugar

The fourth vital ingredient for jam-making and the one that actually preserves the fruit and keeps it from spoiling. In order to do this, the proportion of sugar in a preserve needs to be 60 per cent or higher. Boiling the fruit and sugar mixture drives off water, which helps the sugar content reach this crucial level. Sugar also enhances the flavour of sharp, acidic fruits such as blackcurrants and gooseberries. See Key preserving ingredients, p.35, for in-depth information on different types of sugar.

Setting point

Providing the proportion of ingredients is correct, your jam or jelly should set once it has been sufficiently cooked. There are three simple methods you can use to check if setting point has been reached. Remove the jam from the heat while testing for setting point (it will lose more water as it cooks and may reach a point where it will set too firmly). If setting point has not been reached, return to the boil, cook for a further couple of minutes, then test again.

Crinkle or saucer test Drop a little jam on to a cold saucer (I put one in the fridge when I start jam-making). Allow to cool for a minute then push gently with your fingertip. If the jam crinkles, setting point has been reached.

Flake test Dip a clean wooden spoon into the jam, hold it up over the pan, twirl it around a couple of times, then let the jam drop from the side of it. If the drops run together to form a flake, setting point has been reached.

Temperature test Place a preserving thermometer (see p.41) into the jam when it has reached a rolling boil. When it reads 104.5°C, setting point will have been reached. Pectin-rich fruits will set a degree or two lower.

Making perfect jams and marmalades

This checklist will help to ensure success every time:

1. Always use fresh, dry, slightly under-ripe fruit. Prepare and pick over according to type, i.e. hull strawberries, stone plums, top and tail gooseberries, shred citrus peel. Wash the fruit only if necessary and dry it well.

2. Simmer the fruit gently in a large, uncovered pan before adding the sugar. This softens the fruit and helps draw out the pectin. Soft fruits, such as raspberries and strawberries, will not need added water but tougher-skinned or semi-hard fruits, such as currants, gooseberries, plums, apples and citrus fruit, will.

3. Make sure that the fruit skins are well softened before sugar is added. Once the sugar is in, the skins will not soften further, no matter how long you cook them. Citrus peel for marmalade takes 1½–2 hours to soften.

4. A knob of butter (20g for every 1kg fruit) or a little cooking oil, added at the same time as the sugar, helps to prevent any scum forming on the jam.

5. After adding the sugar to the fruit or juice, stir it over a gentle heat to ensure it is completely dissolved before the mixture begins to boil. Adding the sugar before the jam is boiling helps to 'hold' the fruit in whole or chunky pieces. Warming the sugar in a low oven will speed up the dissolving process, but is not strictly necessary.

6. Once the sugar is dissolved, cook the jam, without stirring, at a full rolling boil, i.e. when the surface is covered by a mass of foamy bubbles that don't recede when stirred. Time your cooking from the point at which the rolling boil begins. Don't stir at this stage – it cools the jam so it would take longer to reach setting point.

7. Test for setting point, using one of the methods given on p.49, when the foamy bubbles have subsided and the boiling surface of the jam appears glossy and heavy.

8. When setting point is reached, remove the pan from the heat. To remove scum, stir the jam (always in the same direction so as not to introduce too much air) until it has dispersed. Alternatively, skim off scum with a slotted spoon. (Scum, by the way, is nothing to worry about – it's just air bubbles created by the intense cooking process.)

9. Allow jams with large pieces of fruit, and thick-cut marmalades, to cool for 10–12 minutes before potting. This allows the mixture to thicken slightly so that the fruit, when potted, should remain well distributed throughout the jar.

10. Pour into clean, sterilised jars (see p.29) while the preserve is still very hot (always above 85°C). Seal with suitable lids and, once cool, store in a cool, dry place.

Making perfect jellies

You will need to prepare the fruit in the same way as for jams (see left), but there are different watchpoints for jelly-making:

1. Soften the fruit by simmering it very gently for 45–60 minutes. With juicy fruits, like strawberries, raspberries, redcurrants and blackberries, allow 300–400ml water per 1kg fruit. For plums and damsons, allow 600ml per 1kg, and for blackcurrants 900ml per 1kg. Apples, quinces and hard fruits should be just covered with water.

2. Strain the cooked fruit pulp through a scalded jelly bag (this helps to make the jelly clear, see p.41) for at least 2 hours or overnight.

3. If you can't resist squeezing or poking the bag to extract more juice, be prepared for your jelly to be cloudy.

4. Allow 450g sugar for every 600ml juice. Bring the juice slowly to the boil and add the sugar only when boiling – this helps to keep your jelly clear and bright: the longer the sugar is cooked, the more the jelly will darken. Boiling time will be somewhere between 5 and 15 minutes, depending on the type of fruit used.

5. Test for a set in the same way as for jam.

6. Skim the jelly and pour into jars as quickly as possible.

Seville orange marmalade

The bitter Seville orange is the most traditional and arguably the finest marmalade fruit of all. Only available for a few short weeks from mid-January, this knobbly, often misshapen orange has a unique aromatic quality and is very rich in pectin. However, you can use almost any citrus fruit to make good marmalade – consider sweet oranges, ruby-red or blood oranges, grapefruit, limes, clementines, kumquats, or a combination of two or three (see my suggested variations overleaf).

There are two basic ways of making marmalade. My first choice is the sliced fruit method, which involves cutting the raw peel into shreds before cooking. I find this technique produces a brighter, clearer result. However, the whole fruit method, in which the fruit is boiled whole before being cut up, is easier and less time-consuming. It tends to create a darker, less delicate preserve – but that, of course, might be exactly what you want. I've given you both methods here …

Sliced fruit method

Makes 5–6 x 450g jars
1kg Seville oranges
75ml lemon juice
2kg demerara sugar

Scrub the oranges, remove the buttons at the top of the fruit, then cut in half. Squeeze out the juice and keep to one side. Using a sharp knife, slice the peel, pith and all, into thin, medium or chunky shreds, according to your preference. Put the sliced peel into a bowl with the orange juice and cover with 2.5 litres water. Leave to soak overnight or for up to 24 hours.

Transfer the whole mixture to a preserving pan, bring to the boil then simmer slowly, covered, until the peel is tender. This should take approximately 2 hours, by which time the contents of the pan will have reduced by about one-third.

Stir in the lemon juice and sugar. Bring the marmalade to the boil, stirring until the sugar has dissolved. Boil rapidly until setting point is reached (see p.49), about 20–25 minutes. Remove from the heat. Leave to cool for 8–10 minutes – a little longer if the peel is in very chunky pieces – then stir gently to disperse any scum, pour into warm, sterilised jars (see p.29) and seal immediately. Use within 2 years.

Whole fruit method

Makes 5 x 450g jars
1kg Seville oranges
75ml lemon juice
2kg granulated sugar

Scrub the fruit, remove the buttons at the top and put it, whole, into a preserving pan with 2.5 litres water. Bring to the boil then simmer, covered, for 2–2½ hours or until the orange skins are tender and can be pierced easily with a fork.

When cool enough to handle, take the oranges out. Measure and keep the cooking water – you should have about 1.7 litres. Make it up to this amount with more water if you have less, or bring to the boil and reduce if you have more.

Cut the oranges in half and remove the pips with a fork, flicking them into a bowl. Strain any juice from the pips back into the cooking water, then discard the pips.

Meanwhile, cut up the orange peel and flesh into thick, medium or thin shreds. Put the cut-up fruit into the strained cooking liquid. Add the lemon juice and sugar and bring to the boil, stirring until the sugar has completely dissolved. Bring to a rolling boil and boil rapidly until setting point is reached (see p.49), about 10–15 minutes.

Leave to cool for 10–12 minutes – a little longer if you've cut the peel into very chunky pieces – then stir gently to disperse any scum, pour into warm, sterilised jars (see p.29) and seal immediately. Use within 2 years.

Variations

You can use both methods for making many other delicious marmalades:

Lemon marmalade with honey Use 1kg lemons instead of oranges, and omit the extra lemon juice. Replace 250g of the sugar with honey, adding it at the same time.

Three-fruit marmalade Use a mixture of grapefruit, lemons and sweet oranges to make up a total of 1kg fruit.

Seville and ginger marmalade Replace 250g of the sugar with 250g chopped crystallised stem ginger, adding it along with the sugar.

Whisky marmalade Add 50ml whisky to the marmalade at the end of cooking.

'Ruby red' marmalade Both pink grapefruits and blood oranges make wonderful marmalades, though I prefer to use the sliced fruit method for these fruits. Add 100ml freshly squeezed lemon juice to every 1kg of fruit.

P.S. Don't limit marmalade to the breakfast table, for its traits and qualities can be well used in other culinary ways. I like to replace candied peel in fruit cakes with a tablespoonful or two of marmalade, and always add some to my Christmas mincemeat (see p.82). Marmalade makes a marvellous glaze for oven-baked ham, as well as sweet and sour chicken or pork dishes. Best of all, 3 or 4 tablespoonfuls will make a glorious golden topping for a good old-fashioned steamed pud.

P.P.S. For generations, marmalade-makers have cooked up the mass of pips found inside citrus fruits in the belief that they are full of pectin. However, most of the pectin is actually found in the citrus peel and I rely purely on this for the setting power in my marmalades.

Early rhubarb jam

Season: mid-January to late March

Early or 'forced' rhubarb has been produced in West Yorkshire since the 1870s, as growers discovered that the heavy clay soil and cold winter climate suited the plant (a native of Siberia). In the 'Rhubarb Triangle' between Bradford, Wakefield and Leeds, the tradition continues to this day. Sequestered in dark sheds, carefully cultivated rhubarb 'crowns' send forth slender, bright-pink stems, much more delicate in flavour than the thick green shafts of outdoor-grown rhubarb that appear later in the year.

This is one of my favourite ways to capture the earthy flavour of rhubarb. It's a plant that contains very little pectin so the jam definitely requires an extra dose. The shortish boil time helps to preserve the fabulous colour of the stems. I like to add a little Seville orange juice, but juice from sweet oranges works well too.

This light, soft jam is good mixed with yoghurt or spooned over ice cream, or you can warm it and use to glaze a bread and butter pudding after baking.

Makes 5 x 340g jars
1kg forced rhubarb (untrimmed weight)
900g jam sugar with added pectin

100ml freshly squeezed Seville or sweet orange juice

Wipe and trim the rhubarb and cut into 2–2.5cm chunks. Pour a layer of sugar into the bottom of a preserving pan, then add a layer of rhubarb. Repeat, continuing until all the sugar and rhubarb are used, finishing with a layer of sugar. Pour the orange juice over the top. Cover and leave for at least an hour or two – preferably overnight. This draws the juice from the rhubarb and the resulting syrup helps keep the rhubarb chunks whole when boiled.

Gently bring the mixture to the boil, stirring carefully without crushing the rhubarb pieces. Boil rapidly for 5–6 minutes, then test for setting point (see p.49).

Remove from the heat and rest for 5 minutes before pouring into warm, sterilised jars (see p.29). Seal immediately (see p.30). Use within 12 months.

Variations
Add 100g chopped crystallised stem ginger to the fruit, omitting the orange juice. Sharper-tasting maincrop rhubarb can also be used for this recipe – try adding a few young angelica leaves or a handful of fragrant rose petals.

Green gooseberry jam
with elderflower

Season: late May to June

I welcome the first tiny gooseberries that appear in the month of May, just as the first boughs of elderflower are beginning to show. The berries are picked when no bigger than my little thumbnail, almost as a thinning process, allowing their brothers and sisters to fill out and mature on the bush. But these early green goddesses are full of pectin, sharp and tart, and make a divine jam. The fragrant elderflowers add a flavour which will remind you, when the days are short and dark, that summer will come again.

Makes 5–6 x 340g jars
1kg young gooseberries
Around 8 heads of elderflower
1kg granulated sugar

Top and tail the gooseberries (it's easiest to just do this with a pair of scissors) and put into a preserving pan with 500ml water. Check the elderflower heads for any insects, then place on top of the gooseberries. Cook gently until the berries are soft but still hold their shape. Remove the elderflowers.

Add the sugar. Stir carefully, so as not to break up the fruit, until the sugar has dissolved, then bring to a full rolling boil and boil for 9–10 minutes. Test for setting point (see p.49).

Remove from the heat, allow to rest for 10 minutes, then pot and seal (see p.30). Use within 12 months.

Variation
Use this recipe for later-season gooseberries, without the elderflowers. The fruit will be sweeter and the jam will have a soft pink colour.

P.S. To make a quick and easy piquant gooseberry sauce to go with mackerel, add a little cider or balsamic vinegar to warmed gooseberry jam (with or without elderflower). Let the flavours mix and mingle before spooning over the barbecued or grilled fish.

Strawberry jam

Season: May to August

After a dismal result with my strawberry jam at the 2007 Uplyme and Lyme Regis Horticultural Show, I decided to get my act together and work out a recipe that I could rely on to get me that much coveted first prize next time. My kitchen soon took on the appearance of a strawberry jam factory, with coded batches piled just about everywhere. I thought I'd nearly made the grade on batch three, but the tweaking for batch four caused mayhem in the jam pan. However, batch five seemed to come alive from the moment the lemon juice was added and I knew it was going to be just right – bright in colour with some soft whole fruit and, of course, that wonderful, intense strawberry taste.

Strawberries are low in pectin. Using sugar with added pectin helps to attain a lovely set and a flavour that isn't too sickly-sweet. Use freshly picked, dry fruit – not too big, or they'll blow to bits when the jam is bubbling away. However, if you're using very small fruit, make sure they're not too hard and seedy.

Makes 4–5 x 340g jars
1kg strawberries, hulled, large
    ones halved or quartered
500g granulated sugar

450g jam sugar with added pectin
150ml lemon juice

Put 200g of the strawberries into a preserving pan with 200g of the granulated sugar. Crush to a pulp with a potato masher. Place the pan on a gentle heat and, when the fruit mixture is warm, add the rest of the strawberries. Very gently bring to simmering point, agitating the bottom of the pan with a wooden spoon to prevent the fruit from sticking. Simmer for 5 minutes to allow the strawberries to soften just a little.

Add the remaining granulated sugar and the jam sugar. Stir gently to prevent the sugar sticking and burning on the bottom of the pan. When the sugar has dissolved, add the lemon juice. Increase the heat and, when the mixture reaches a full boil, boil rapidly for 8–9 minutes. Then test for setting point (see p.49).

Remove from the heat and, if the surface is scummy, stir gently until the scum has dispersed. Pot and seal (see p.30). Use within 12 months.

Redcurrant jelly

Season: June to mid-July

Redcurrants make a superb and very versatile jelly. In addition, their juice can be turned into a delicious alcoholic cordial (p.144). The redcurrant season is short, just a few weeks in midsummer, so make sure you don't miss it. If you haven't time to make your jelly straight away, you can pick the currants and freeze for later.

This is an endlessly useful jelly. A classic tracklement to accompany roast lamb or game, you can also use it to enhance the flavour of gravies, casseroles and piquant sauces. It makes an excellent glaze for fresh fruit tarts too.

Makes 4–5 x 225g jars
1kg redcurrants
Granulated sugar

You don't have to top and tail the currants, or even take them off their stalks. Simply wash them, put into a preserving pan with 400ml water, then simmer until they are very soft and have released all their juice. This will take about 45 minutes. Strain through a jelly bag (see p.41) for several hours, or overnight. Do not poke, squeeze or force the pulp through the bag or you'll get a cloudy jelly.

Measure the juice, put into the cleaned preserving pan and bring to the boil. For every 600ml juice add 450g sugar, adding it only when the juice is boiling. Stir until the sugar has dissolved, ensuring the sides of the pan are free of undissolved sugar crystals. Then boil rapidly for about 8 minutes or until setting point is reached (see p.49).

Remove from the heat and stir to disperse any scum, then pour into warm, sterilised jars and seal (see p.30). Tap the jars to disperse any air bubbles caught in the jelly. Use within 12 months.

Variation
Add a couple of tablespoonfuls of chopped fresh mint to the redcurrant jelly for the last 2–3 minutes of boiling.

P.S. Redcurrant jelly is the core ingredient of Cumberland sauce, a traditional partner to baked ham and game. Just add 50ml port, the grated zest of 1 orange and 1 lemon, 1 tsp cayenne pepper, a pinch or two of mustard powder and perhaps a pinch of ground ginger to 200g redcurrant jelly.

Mum's blackcurrant jam

Season: June to August

In my jam company days, when we would produce nearly 15,000 jars of preserves each week, my mum would still bring me jars of her home-made blackcurrant jam. Sometimes I wondered if I needed another jar in the house, but I always enjoyed it immensely – blackcurrant jam is an all-time favourite, with a flavour that is rarely rivalled. It's also very easy to make. The key is to ensure that the blackcurrants are softened sufficiently before the sugar is added, or the skins will toughen and be unpleasantly chewy.

Use this in all the usual jammy ways with bread, toast, pancakes, yoghurt, rice pudding, cakes, tarts and, of course, scones and clotted cream.

Makes 7–8 x 340g jars
1kg blackcurrants
1.5kg golden granulated sugar

Pick over the blackcurrants, removing any stalks, twiggy bits or damaged fruit (the dry shrivelled bit at one end is the remains of the flower and need not be removed).

Put the currants into a preserving pan with 600ml water. Place over a low heat and slowly bring to simmering point. Simmer for 15–20 minutes, or until the fruit is soft but not disintegrated into a pulp.

Add the sugar and stir until it has dissolved. Then bring quickly to a full rolling boil. Boil hard for 5 minutes. Remove from the heat and continue to stir gently for a couple of minutes to reduce the temperature. Test for setting point (see p.49).

Let the jam cool a little and make sure the currants aren't bobbing above the surface when you pour it into warm, sterilised jam jars (see p.29). If they are, then let the jam cool a little longer, and if they really won't submerge, then bring the pan back to the boil and boil for a couple more minutes.

P.S. The bittersweet leaves of the blackcurrant bush can be used as a substitute for tea. Simply infuse the leaves in boiling water, leave for 10 minutes then serve sweetened with a little honey.

Hugh's prize-winning
raspberry fridge jam

Season: June to October

Hugh F-W, whose recipe this is, thinks the secret of success is to pick the raspberries on a hot, dry day, aiming for a good mixture of ripe and almost-ripe fruit, then to make the jam immediately – to capture the full flavour of the berries.

The light boiling and lower-than-normal quantity of sugar produce a loose, soft-set jam with a fresh, tangy flavour. Low-sugar jams of this type are often called fridge jams (see p.44). In fact, as long as it is capped when still above 90°C, this preserve will keep well in the store cupboard. However, once it is opened, you must keep it in the fridge. It won't last long after opening – maybe 2 or 3 weeks – but as it tastes so very, very good, this is unlikely to be a problem. It's one of those things you'll find yourself eating straight from the jar, maybe in the middle of the night!

This light, soft jam is fantastic in cakes or sherry trifles or stirred into creamy rice puddings. Best of all, layer it with toasted oatmeal, cream, Drambuie and honey for a take on the traditional Scottish pudding, cranachan.

Makes 6 x 340g jars
1.5kg raspberries
750g jam sugar with added pectin

Start by picking over the raspberries very carefully and discarding any leaves or stalks. Put half the fruit into a preserving pan and use a potato masher to roughly crush it. Add the remaining fruit and sugar (the mixture will look mouth-wateringly good).

Stir over a low heat to dissolve the sugar. Bring to a rolling boil then boil for exactly 5 minutes. (If you prefer a firmer jam, then continue boiling at this stage for a further 2–3 minutes). Remove from the heat, stirring to disperse any scum.

It is important to pour and cap this low-sugar jam quickly (see p.30), but you must allow it to cool just a little first (give it 5–6 minutes) to prevent all those little raspberry pips rushing to the top of the jar, leaving you with half a jar of raspberry jelly and half a jar of raspberry pips.

Variation
Flavourful ripe strawberries give very good results with this simple recipe too. Hull the strawberries, halve or quarter larger ones and continue as above.

Plum jam

Plums make a lovely jam and are rich in pectin and easy to prepare, so this is a great recipe for beginners. Just make sure the plums are tender and their skins well softened before adding the sugar. If not, the sugar hardens the skins and they'll be tough in the finished jam; they will also float to the top of the jar.

The widely available 'Victoria' is a first-rate jam plum but you can make a good preserve with others, including 'Early Rivers', 'Czar' and the yellow, egg-like 'Pershore', as well as greengages and smaller hedgerow plums such as bullaces and damsons.

Makes 8 x 340g jars
1.5kg plums
1.25kg granulated sugar

Halve and stone the plums. Crack a few of the stones open, using nutcrackers, and extract the kernels. Put these into a basin and cover with boiling water. Leave for a minute or so, then drain them and rub off the reddish-brown skin. The kernels will add a lovely almond-like flavour to the jam.

Put the plums, skinned kernels and 400ml water into a preserving pan. Bring to a simmer and cook gently until the fruit is tender and the skins soft – this should take about 20 minutes but depends on the variety and size of plum.

Add the sugar and stir until dissolved. Bring to boiling point and boil rapidly until setting point is reached (see p.49), usually 10–12 minutes. Remove from the heat. If the fruit is bobbing about at the surface, it's probably not cooked well enough (the sugar is heavier than the plums, and the jam must cook sufficiently for the fruit to absorb the sugar). If this happens, boil for a further 2–4 minutes.

Pot the jam and cover (see p.30). Use within 12 months.

Variations
Replace some of the water with freshly squeezed orange juice and/or add 2 cinnamon sticks. Another nice twist is to add 100g chopped walnuts to the jam towards the end of the boiling time.

Apple, herb and flower jellies

Season: late summer to autumn

The aromatic essences of fresh herbs and flowers can be captured beautifully in a jelly. These preserves are great to have in the kitchen as they add a sweet piquancy to all kinds of food, simple and rich. Cooking apples and crab apples are both ideal choices for the basic jelly. Excellent sources of pectin and acid, they nevertheless have gentle flavours that will not overwhelm the herbs.

Serve mint jelly with lamb, sage with fish, basil with poultry or game, parsley with ham or gammon, and rose-petal jelly (see below) with wafer-thin bread and butter. Any herb jelly will also be delicious with soft cheeses, pâtés and terrines.

Makes 5–6 x 225g jars

1.5kg cooking apples	Granulated sugar
1 medium bunch of sage, rosemary, mint, tarragon, thyme or basil	100ml cider vinegar

Roughly chop the apples, discarding any bad parts, but don't peel or core them. Place in a preserving pan with the herbs, reserving half a dozen small sprigs to put into the jars. Barely cover the apples with water. Bring to the boil then simmer gently, covered, for 45 minutes to 1 hour, until the fruit is very soft. Tip the contents of the pan into a jelly bag or piece of muslin suspended over a bowl (see p.41) and leave to drip for at least 2 hours, or overnight.

Measure the strained juice. For every 600ml, weigh out 450g sugar. Return the juice to the cleaned-out pan, with the vinegar. Heat to boiling point then add the sugar and stir until dissolved. Increase the heat and boil rapidly for 10–12 minutes or until setting point is reached (see p.49). Remove from the heat and skim with a slotted spoon to remove any scum.

Pour into small, warm, sterilised jars (see p.29), adding a herb sprig to each. Cover and seal (see p.30). Use within 12 months.

Variations

For stronger-flavoured jellies, you can add 3–4 tbsp freshly chopped herbs after removing the jelly from the heat. Allow to cool for 10 minutes before potting. For exquisite rose-petal or dandelion jelly, add 25g scented petals instead of herbs. The above method can also be used to make quince and medlar jellies, replacing the apples with your chosen fruit and leaving out the herbs.

Blackberry and apple leather

Season: late August to September

Fruit leathers are thin, pliable sheets of dried, sweetened fruit purée with a flexible consistency exactly like leather. To be truthful, I had always avoided making them, thinking they sounded complicated. But, in a spirit of experimentation, I decided to try some out for this book. They were a revelation. I discovered how easy it is to create these strong, semi-transparent sheets, and how versatile they are. They are fun to use and eat – you can cut them, roll them, fold them and pack them away. Light and easy to carry, they're full of fruity energy, so great for lunch boxes or long walks. Snip off pieces to dissolve gently into fruit salads, or save them for the festive season when their translucent, jewel-like colours will look gorgeous on the Christmas tree.

Makes 2 sheets of 24 x 30cm
500g blackberries
500g peeled, cored and chopped
    cooking apples (2–3 large apples)

Juice of 1 lemon
150g honey

Preheat the oven to a very low setting – I use 60°C/Gas Mark ⅛ (approximately). Line two baking sheets, measuring about 24 x 30cm, with baking parchment.

Put the blackberries, apples and lemon juice into a pan. Cook gently until soft and pulpy, about 20 minutes. Rub the mixture through a sieve or mouli into a bowl; you should have about 700g smooth fruit purée. Add the honey and mix well.

Divide the purée between the two baking sheets. Spread it out lightly with the back of a spoon until the purée covers the sheets in a thin, even layer.

Put the baking sheets in the oven and leave for 12–18 hours, until the fruit purée is completely dry and peels off the parchment easily. Roll up the leather in greaseproof paper and store in an airtight tin. Use within 5 months.

Variations
There is no end to the possible variations here – you can turn any fruit into a leather. All you need do is create a smooth, thick purée with your chosen fruit before drying it out. Try plums, spicing the purée with a little cinnamon; or peaches, infusing them with a few honeysuckle blossoms as they cook. For a savoury leather use half and half apples and tomatoes seasoned with 2 tsp souper mix (see p.207) or celery salt.

Bramley lemon curd

Season: late August to January

When I made preserves for a living, I tried all kinds of curds, from orange to passion fruit, but none of them was ever quite as popular as the good old-fashioned lemon variety. I didn't think I could improve on it until recently, when I came across an old recipe for an appley lemon curd. I tried it out and I now prefer it even to a classic straight lemon curd – it's like eating apples and custard: softly sweet, tangy and quite, quite delicious.

Makes 5 x 225g jars

450g Bramley apples, peeled, cored and chopped

Finely grated zest and juice of 2 unwaxed lemons (you need 100ml strained juice)

125g unsalted butter

450g granulated sugar

4–5 large eggs, well beaten (you need 200ml beaten egg)

Put the chopped apples into a pan with 100ml water and the lemon zest. Cook gently until soft and fluffy, then either beat to a purée with a wooden spoon or rub through a nylon sieve.

Put the butter, sugar, lemon juice and apple purée into a double boiler or heatproof bowl over a pan of simmering water. As soon as the butter has melted and the mixture is hot and glossy, pour in the eggs through a sieve, and whisk with a balloon whisk. If the fruit purée is too hot when the beaten egg is added, the egg will 'split'. One way to guard against this is to check the temperature of the purée with a sugar thermometer – it should be no higher than 55–60°C when the egg is added. If your curd does split, take the pan off the heat and whisk vigorously until smooth.

Stir the mixture over a gentle heat, scraping down the sides of the bowl every few minutes, until thick and creamy. This will take 9–10 minutes; the temperature should reach 82–84°C on a sugar thermometer. Immediately pour into warm, sterilised jars (see p.29) and seal (see p.30). Use within 4 weeks. Once opened, keep in the fridge.

Variations

To make gooseberry curd, replace the apples with gooseberries. If you'd like to go for a traditional, pure lemon curd, simply leave out the apples, increase the lemon juice to 200ml (4–5 lemons) and add the grated zest of 2–3 lemons.

Hedgerow jelly

Season: September to October

The months of September and October allow us to reap the berried treasure of the hedgerows – a seasonal activity that is not without its dangers as many wild fruits are guarded by all sorts of thorns, prickles and entangling stems. However, with a little common sense and determination you should be able to overcome these country hurdles, and the basketful of fruit you bring home will be a just reward.

At the heart of all the best hedgerow jellies is the crab apple (*Malus sylvestris*). The pectin in this often scarred and scabby pomaceous fruit lends the setting power that many hedgerow berries lack. Crab apples produce a stunning pink jelly when used on their own, too.

For this recipe, you can use crab apples, sloes, bullaces, hips, haws, blackberries, elderberries or rowan berries. Usually, I go for about 50 per cent crab apples with a combination of two or three different berries. If I've gathered rosehips or rowan berries, however, I prefer to use them on their own, blended only with crab apple (see the variations overleaf).

Makes 7–8 x 225g jars
1kg crab apples (or cooking apples)
1kg mixed hedgerow berries (see above)
Around 900g granulated sugar

Pick over your fruit, removing stalks and leafy bits and rinsing the berries if necessary. Don't peel or core the apples (the peel and core are an excellent source of pectin), just chop them roughly. Place all the prepared fruit in a saucepan with 1.2 litres water. Bring gently to simmering point and simmer until all the fruit is soft and pulpy. Remove from the heat.

Have ready a scalded jelly bag or muslin cloth (see p.41) and turn the contents of the pan into it. Leave to drip overnight. The jelly will turn cloudy if you squeeze the juice through so just let it drip at its own pace.

The next day, measure the juice – you will probably have about 1.2 litres, though this will depend on the berries used. For every 600ml juice, allow 450g sugar. Put the juice into a large pan and bring slowly to the boil. Add the sugar as it just comes to the boil and keep stirring until the sugar has dissolved. Then boil rapidly, without stirring, for 9–10 minutes until setting point is reached (see p.49). Skim the jelly and pot and seal as quickly as possible (see p.30). Use within 12 months.

Variations

These are some of my favourite takes on the hedgerow jelly idea. In each case, follow the hedgerow jelly method and quantities (on the previous page); i.e. always use 450g sugar to each 600ml strained fruit juice.

Spicy crab apple jelly Use crab apples alone and add a few cloves and a couple of cinnamon sticks when the fruit is being cooked. This all-time classic hedgerow jelly is equally at home on thinly sliced hot buttered toast or as an accompaniment to succulent cold roast pork or turkey.

Rosehip and apple jelly Use 500g rosehips, first blitzed in a food processor, and 1.5kg crab or cooking apples. Excellent with roast pork.

Rowan jelly Use 1kg rowan berries and 1kg crab apples. Add the juice of 1 lemon before adding the sugar. For a really aromatic jelly, add a bunch of sage or thyme when the fruit is softening. Rowan jelly is lovely served with game.

Blackberry and apple jelly Use 1kg blackberries and 1kg apples. This is a nostalgic teatime treat for me, as I remember how good my grandmother's blackberry and apple jelly always tasted on wafer-thin slices of bread and butter.

P.S. Hedgerow jelly, or any other well-coloured jelly, can be used as a natural colouring for glacé icing. Just a teaspoonful or two will be sufficient to give your icing a wickedly deep hue that will be sure to liven up your cakes.

Honeyed hazels

Season: September

You've got to be quick to beat the squirrels to the hazelnuts each autumn. Once you've managed to find some, it's important to store them carefully. Even with their shells on, they have a tendency to dry out and shrivel up, but preserving them in honey will keep them fresh and fragrant for ages. Use wild hazels that you have gathered yourself, or British-grown cobnuts – which are simply a cultivated form of hazelnut.

Spoon your honeyed hazels over plain yoghurt, chocolate ice cream, porridge or muesli. They're also delicious as a topping for a steamed sponge pudding.

Makes 2 x 225g jars
500g hazelnuts or cobnuts
340g clear honey

Start by inviting your friends round for a nut-cracking evening (they'll come the first year, but maybe not the next). Crack all the nuts and remove the kernels.

Heat a frying pan over a low heat. Toast the shelled nuts in batches for 4–5 minutes, jiggling and shaking the pan to make sure they don't burn. Remove from the heat and allow to cool.

Pack the nuts into sterilised jars (see p.29), adding 1 tbsp honey at every third or fourth layer. Continue until the jars are chock-a-block full, making sure that the nuts are well covered in honey. Seal securely with a lid and store in a cool, dry, dark place. Use within 12 months.

P.S. 'Clear' honey is runny while 'set' honey is thick and opaque, but apart from this there is no real difference between the two types – it's just down to the feeding ground for the bees. Borage honey, a speciality of east Yorkshire, is one of the clearest honeys you will ever come across, whereas clover honey is favoured for its creamy thick texture and floral flavour. All honey, with the exception of heather honey, will eventually become cloudy as a result of the natural process of crystallisation. If you find this happens and you want your honey to be runny again, then just stand the jar in a bowl of hot water for a few minutes until it is liquid honey again.

Plum and russet mincemeat

Season: September to October

The term 'mincemeat' originated in the fifteenth century, when chopped meat was preserved with a combination of dried fruit, sugar and aromatic spices. During the seventeenth century, beef or lamb suet replaced the meat and has been used ever since – with vegetarian 'suet' a more recent option. This recipe is a departure on several fronts: it uses fresh fruit as well as dried, and contains no suet. In fact, it contains very little fat (only the oil in the walnuts). The result is light and fruity, but with all the rich, warm spiciness of a traditional mincemeat.

Makes 4 x 450g jars

1kg plums
Finely grated zest and juice of 2–3
    oranges (you need 200ml juice)
500g russet apples, peeled, cored and
    chopped into 1cm cubes
200g currants
200g raisins
200g sultanas

100g orange marmalade
250g demerara sugar
½ tsp ground cloves
2 tsp ground ginger
½ nutmeg, grated
50ml ginger wine or cordial (optional)
100g chopped walnuts
50ml brandy or sloe gin

Wash the plums, halve and remove the stones, then put into a saucepan with the orange juice. Cook gently until tender, about 15 minutes. Blend to a purée in a liquidiser or push through a sieve. You should end up with about 700ml plum purée.

Put the purée into a large bowl and add all the other ingredients, except the brandy or gin. Mix thoroughly, then cover and leave to stand for 12 hours.

Preheat the oven to 130°C/Gas Mark ½. Put the mincemeat in a large baking dish and bake, uncovered, for 2–2½ hours. Stir in the brandy or gin, then spoon into warm, sterilised jars (see p.29), making sure there aren't any air pockets. Seal (see p.30) and store in a dry, dark, cool place until Christmas. Use within 12 months.

Variations

You can vary this recipe, but keep the fresh fruit purée to around 700ml and the total amount of dried fruit to 600g. For an apple, pear and ginger mincemeat, replace the plums with Bramley apples, the russet apples with firm pears, and 100g of the raisins or sultanas with 100g crystallised stem ginger. You could also exchange the walnuts for almonds and add a couple of teaspoonfuls of ground cinnamon.

Quince cheese

Season: late September to October

A fruit cheese is simply a solid, sliceable preserve – and the princely quince, with its exquisite scent and delicately grainy texture, makes the most majestic one of all. It can be potted in small moulds to turn out, slice and eat with cheese. Alternatively, you can pour it into shallow trays to set, then cut it into cubes, coat with sugar and serve as a sweetmeat.

A little roughly chopped quince cheese adds a delicious fruity note to lamb stews or tagines – or try combining it with chopped apple for a pie or crumble.

Makes about 1kg
1kg quince
500–750g granulated sugar

Food-grade paraffin wax, for sealing
(see the directory, p.210)

Wash the quince. Roughly chop the fruit but don't peel or core them. Place in a large pan and barely cover with water. Bring to a simmer and cook until soft and pulpy, adding a little more water if necessary. Leave to stand for several hours.

Rub the contents of the pan through a sieve or pass through a mouli. Weigh the pulp and return it to the cleaned-out pan, adding an equal weight of sugar. Bring gently to the boil, stirring until the sugar has dissolved, then simmer gently, stirring frequently, for an hour and a bit until really thick and glossy. It may bubble and spit like a volcano, so do take care. The mixture is ready when it is so thick that you can scrape a spoon through it and see the base of the pan for a couple of seconds before the mixture oozes together again.

If you're using small dishes or straight-sided jars, brush them with a little glycerine (see the directory). This will make it easy to turn out the cheese. If you're using a shallow baking tray or similar, line it with greaseproof paper, allowing plenty of overhang to wrap the finished cheese.

When the cheese is cooked, pour it into the prepared moulds or jars. To seal open moulds, pour melted food-grade paraffin wax over the hot fruit cheese. Jars can be sealed with lids. Cheese set in a shallow tray should be covered with greaseproof paper and kept in the fridge.

For optimum flavour, allow the quince cheese to mature for 4–6 weeks before using. Eat within 12 months.

Melissa's chestnut jam

Season: October to December

I first made this deliciously sweet preserve while staying at a farm on Dartmoor. Melissa, who lived at the farm, came to help with the laborious job of peeling the chestnuts, and we whipped through them in no time. The addition of honey to the jam seemed entirely appropriate, since that's what 'Melissa' means in Greek.

I like to spoon chestnut jam into meringue nests and top with cream. Or stir a spoonful or two into chocolate mousse, or dollop on to vanilla ice cream before drizzling with hot chocolate sauce. This preserve also makes a lovely filling for chocolate cakes, and of course, it can be enjoyed simply spread on crusty bread.

Makes 5 x 225g jars

1kg sweet chestnuts
400g granulated sugar
1 tsp vanilla paste or extract
100g honey
50ml brandy

The first task is to remove the leathery shells and skin from the chestnuts. Use a sharp knife to make a knick in the top of each chestnut. Plunge them into a pan of boiling water for 2–3 minutes – sufficient time to soften the shell but not to let the nuts get piping hot and difficult to handle. Remove the pan from the heat. Fish out half a dozen or so chestnuts and peel off their coats. With luck, the thin brown skin under the shell will peel away too. Continue in this way until all are peeled.

Put the chestnuts into a clean pan and just cover with water. Bring to the boil and simmer for 25–30 minutes, or until tender. Strain, but keep the cooking liquid.

Purée the chestnuts with 100ml of the cooking liquid in a food processor or using a stick blender.

Pour a further 100ml of the cooking liquid into a pan and add the sugar. Heat gently until dissolved. Add the chestnut purée, vanilla paste and honey. Stir until well blended. Bring to the boil then cook gently for 5–10 minutes until well thickened. Take care, as it will pop and splutter and may spit. Remove from the heat and stir in the brandy. Pour into warm, sterilised jars (see p.29) and seal immediately (see p.30). Use within 6 months. Store in the fridge once opened.

Candied orange sticks

Season: any time

I like to make several batches of these sweetmeats in November or early December. A dozen or so, wrapped in cellophane, are a charming gift. Needless to say, you don't need to stop at oranges: lemon and grapefruit peel work equally well and you can use milk, plain or white chocolate for dipping. The glucose syrup is optional, but does prevent the sticks becoming too hard. It is best to keep the candied sticks in an airtight container and only dip them in chocolate when you want them.

Makes about 100 sticks
4–5 large oranges
500g granulated sugar

1 tbsp glucose syrup (optional)
200g good plain chocolate

Scrub the oranges then remove the peel in quarters. To do this, cut through the peel with a sharp knife, going right round the orange, starting and finishing at the stalk, then repeat, at right angles to the first cut. Remove the peel, with the attached pith, from the fruit. Weigh out 250g peel and cut it into slices, about 6mm x 5cm.

Put the orange peel slices into a large pan and cover with 2 litres of cold water. Bring to the boil and simmer for 5 minutes. Drain and return to the pan with 1 litre of cold water. Bring to the boil and simmer, covered, for 45 minutes. Add the sugar and stir until dissolved (it won't take long). Simmer, covered, for 30 minutes. Remove from the heat and leave to stand for 24 hours.

Bring the pan to the boil again. Add the glucose syrup if using and boil gently, uncovered, for 30 minutes or until all the liquid has evaporated and the orange sticks are coated with bubbling orange syrup. Remove from the heat and allow to cool. Using a pair of tongs (or your fingers), carefully remove the orange sticks and place on a wire rack (with a tray underneath to catch the drips). Leave in a warm place, such as an airing cupboard, for 24 hours, or place in a very low oven at approximately 60°C/Gas Mark ⅛ for 2–3 hours to dry.

Break the chocolate into pieces, put into a heatproof bowl over a pan of simmering water and leave until melted. Remove from the heat. Dip one half of each orange stick in the melted chocolate and place on a sheet of greaseproof paper to dry.

Before dipping, the sticks will keep well for 3–4 months. Once they have their chocolate coating, they are best eaten within 3 weeks.

Cider apple butter

Season: September to November

Autumn is the season for apples. For centuries, the apple crop has been important and the apple tree cherished and celebrated for its fruit. Wassailing is a West Country tradition when, on Twelfth Night of old (17 January), country folk toast and drink the health of the largest and most prolific apple tree in the orchard for a healthy, fruitful crop the coming season.

The sharp and bittersweet qualities of cider gives this old-fashioned apple butter a special flavour. It's a sensational fruity spread to daub over hot buttered toast or crumpets.

Makes 5–6 x 225g jars
1.5kg cooking apples
600ml dry or medium cider
Granulated sugar

½ tsp ground cloves
½ tsp ground cinnamon

There is no need to peel or core the apples. However, if you are using windfalls (and this is a very good recipe in which to do so), cut away any damaged or bruised bits. Chop the apples into fairly big pieces (each into about 8). Place in a large pan with the cider and 600ml water. Cook gently until soft, then remove from the heat.

Push the apple mixture through a nylon sieve or use a mouli to reduce it to a purée. Weigh the fruit pulp and return it to the cleaned-out pan, adding 340g sugar for every 600ml fruit pulp. Add the cloves and cinnamon. Slowly bring to the boil, stirring until the sugar has dissolved, then boil rapidly for 10–15 minutes until the mixture begins to splutter and is thick and creamy.

Remove from the heat and pour immediately into warm, sterilised jars (see p.29) (it's best to use small jars as this low-sugar preserve has a relatively short shelf life, once opened). Seal immediately (see p.30). Use within 12 months. Store in the fridge once opened.

Variation
Blackberries make a beautiful fruit butter. Follow the above method using 1kg ripe blackberries, 500g cored and peeled cooking apples and 100ml lemon juice; allow 300g sugar for every 600ml fruit pulp.

Compost heap jelly

Season: any time

This is a wonderful, frugal recipe that complements some of the other fruity preserves in the book because it uses the apple scraps and citrus skins that would normally be destined for the compost heap or bin. These skins are full of flavour and rich in pectin, so it's a shame not to use them. For the cost of a bag of sugar (and a bit of your time) you can transform them into a really fruity, marmalade-flavoured jelly. It functions nicely as an emergency breakfast preserve when your last jar of marmalade has been eaten and the seasonal Sevilles haven't yet arrived in the shops.

Makes 3 x 225g jars

500g apple cores and peel
500g citrus fruit peel (unwaxed
    lemon, orange, grapefruit and/or
    lime), cut into roughly 1cm shreds

Granulated sugar
Juice of 1 orange, lemon or grapefruit
    (optional)

Put the apple cores and peel and the citrus peel into a saucepan. Add sufficient water to cover (you'll probably need about 1.5 litres). Bring to a simmer and cook slowly for 45–60 minutes – this softens the fruit and releases the valuable pectin. Turn the fruit into a scalded jelly bag or muslin (see p.41) and leave overnight to drip.

Measure the strained liquid and weigh 450g sugar for every 600ml juice. Return the juice to the pan and add the orange, lemon or grapefruit juice, if using. Bring to the boil, then add the sugar. Stir until dissolved then boil rapidly, without stirring, until setting point is reached (see p.49), about 10 minutes or so.

Remove from the heat and stir, always going in the same direction, until all the surface bubbles have disappeared. Pour into warm, sterilised jars (see p.29) and either swivel or tap the side of the jars to remove any remaining bubbles. Seal in the usual way (see p.30). Use within 12 months.

Pickles, Chutneys
& Relishes

Time for vinegar vapours to fill the air! This chapter is a little sharper than the last one – and full of recipes that feature piquancy, bite and spice. These sweet/sour preserves are generally inexpensive and easy to make. There are only a few guidelines to follow – you don't have to worry about pectin or acid, for instance, as in jam-making. Their uses extend far beyond cold meat and ploughman's lunches. They can be stirred into soups, added to meaty stews, curries or tagines, served with smoked or marinated fish and, of course, combined with other ingredients to make great sandwiches and picnic food. No home should be without them!

Often lumped together, pickles, chutneys and relishes are actually distinctly different and not prepared in the same way:

Clear pickles These are an age-old British way of preserving vegetables or fruit, which are usually left raw or only lightly cooked, and kept whole or in large pieces. Pickles rely predominately on vinegar and salt for keepability though sugar, honey, spices and herbs can all be added for extra flavour. After salting (see p.96), the ingredients are rinsed and drained before being packed into jars and fully covered with plain or spiced vinegar. Pickled onions are the classic example of this type of preserve.

Sweet pickles Made from fruits and vegetables, again in relatively large pieces, lightly cooked in sweetened vinegar, these are often flavoured with spices such as ginger, cloves and allspice. In some recipes – piccalilli, for instance – the vinegar syrup is thickened with cornflour to make a light sauce. The cooked produce is packed in warm jars and the vinegar syrup reduced and poured over the fruit to cover.

Chutneys We learnt about chutney-making from our Indian colonies in the nineteenth century, and authentic Indian chutneys are usually fresh preparations served with spicy foods. The British interpretation of a chutney is rather different: rich, highly spiced, sweet-sharp preserves, based on vegetables and fruit which are chopped small and cooked for a long time to create a spoonable consistency and mellow flavour. They often feature dried fruit too, which contributes natural sugar and textural contrast.

Relishes Somewhere between pickles and chutneys, these are made from diced or chunkily cut fruit and vegetables but they are cooked for a shorter time than a chutney. They can be spicy, sweet, sour (or all three), may be eaten soon after making and should be kept in the fridge once opened.

Essential ingredients

Pickles and chutneys customarily rely on vinegar or a mix of vinegar, salt and/or sugar to preserve tender, young vegetables and fruit. Highly flavoured spices or herbs are added to augment the final flavour, but their often fiery potency will mellow as the preserve matures.

Salt

This plays a very important role in pickling and chutney-making and, indeed, can be used as the sole preservative, as in preserved lemons (p.126). However, it's more usually employed as a general flavour enhancer, and in the preparation of vegetables and fruit prior to pickling. It may be sprinkled straight on to the ingredients (this is known as dry-salting) or made into a brine (wet-salting) in which the ingredients are immersed and left for 12–24 hours. The salt firms up the vegetables and removes excess water which would otherwise dilute the vinegar and cause the pickle to turn mouldy. Dry-salting is ideal for watery vegetables such as cucumbers and marrows, and for very crisp pickles, whereas brine is less harsh and can be used for less juicy produce. A fine-grained salt is essential for dry-salting as it will adhere closely to the surface of the ingredient, but any good-quality salt can be used in a brine. See p.38 for more information on different types of salt.

To make brine For a good all-purpose brine, allow 50g salt to 600ml water (a lighter brine is more appropriate for small ingredients such as nasturtium seeds). Simply dissolve the salt in the water and the brine is ready to use. The prepared ingredients should be covered with the brine and left overnight or for up to 24 hours, before being drained, dried, packed and pickled in jars. Many old recipes call for the brine to be 'strong enough to float an egg'; you will find this ratio will do just that.

To dry-salt Layer your cut-up vegetables on a shallow dish, sprinkling fine salt between each layer. As in brining, the vegetables are left overnight or for up to 24 hours. After a few hours, you will see water being drawn from the vegetables. After salting, the ingredients need to be rinsed in very cold water (to keep them crisp), drained well and patted dry before being pickled.

Vinegar

Your pickles and chutneys will only be as good as the vinegar you use. If vinegar is the main preserving ingredient, as in most of the following recipes, it's important to use a good-quality variety with at least 5 per cent acetic acid content (you should find this information on the bottle). Beyond that, there are no hard and fast rules as to the type of vinegar you should go for – it's very much a matter of taste (see p.37 for more information on different types). However, in general, a translucent vinegar gives a better appearance in a clear pickle.

The vinegar used for pickling is almost always spiced. You can buy ready-spiced 'pickling vinegars', commonly based on malt vinegar. However, I prefer to make my own at home, so I can choose the type of vinegar and the precise spice mix.

Spices

These are essential to give fiery bite, flavour and aroma to pickles and chutneys. Whole spices are used for pickles – ground ones produce a cloudy result – but either whole or freshly ground spices can be used for chutneys. Whole spices should be tied in a muslin bag or enclosed in a tea or spice infuser (see the directory, p.210) so they can be easily removed after cooking.

To make a muslin spice bag, cut a piece of muslin, about 20cm square, put the spices in a heap in the middle and gather up the edges of the muslin to form a little sack. Tie the bag with string so that the spices are loosely but securely held in.

A traditional pickling spice blend can be bought ready-mixed but you'll get a much fresher flavour if you make up your own – I generally combine equal quantities of cinnamon stick, whole cloves, mace blades, whole allspice and a few peppercorns and allow 15–30g of this mix for every 1 litre of vinegar. I like to add a good tablespoonful of demerara sugar and a couple of fresh bay leaves when I brew up the spice. The mix can be kept in an airtight jar for at least a year and used as required. Other spices such as bruised root ginger, fresh or dried chillies, and fennel, dill or celery seeds can also be added to bring a different range of flavours to your pickles.

Always check the sell-by date on your spices and be ruthless about getting rid of any that are past their best. Once they reach a certain age, they'll lose the aroma and flavour you need. If you are using ground spice in a recipe, it is always worth taking the time to grind your own because, once ground, spices lose their pungency amazingly quickly. Give whole spices a light toasting in a dry frying pan then grind as finely as possible in a pestle and mortar, or a spice or coffee grinder. Prepare the spices in small quantities and don't keep the mix for more than a week or two.

Vegetables and fruit

These ingredients, which will make up the bulk and body of your preserve, should be young, firm and as fresh as possible. Almost any produce can be used, though soft berries are generally better in jams and jellies. I've made pickles and chutneys with just about everything else! Apples, gooseberries, pears, plums, marrows and tomatoes (ripe or green) form the base of most chutneys. For most recipes they should be peeled, washed and well drained, before being chopped, diced or left whole. Cut away any bruised or damaged flesh – this will not improve your pickles.

Making perfect pickles

Pickles are very easy to make and their success relies quite simply on good preparation of the raw ingredients, a well-spiced vinegar and an adequate maturing period.

1. After brining or salting your prepared fruit or vegetables, rinse and drain them well.

2. To prevent bruising, don't pack the produce too tightly into the jars.

3. Pack in an attractive way to within 2.5cm of the top of the jar, leaving enough room for the contents to be completely covered with vinegar.

4. Always use sterilised jars (see p.29) and vinegar-proof lids (see the directory, p.210).

5. Use cold vinegar for crisp pickles and hot vinegar if a softer texture is required.

6. Store your pickles in a cool, dark, dry place and leave them for at least 4 weeks before using.

Making perfect chutneys

Don't rush your chutney-making, for a good chutney will take several hours to make. The end result will be more than worthy of the time you've spent.

1. Use a stainless-steel pan and wooden spoon – other materials may react with the vinegar and cause discoloration.

2. Cut fruit and vegetables into small, even-sized pieces – this is time-consuming but really crucial in achieving a good final texture.

3. Long, slow cooking in an open pan is essential for the chutney to become rich, smooth and mellow.

4. Towards the end of cooking, stir frequently so the chutney doesn't catch on the bottom of the pan.

5. The chutney has reached the right consistency when you can draw a wooden spoon across the bottom of the pan and see a clear line for a few seconds before the chutney comes together again.

6. Fill jars to within 5mm of the top and cover with vinegar-proof lids. Badly covered chutney will dry out and shrink in the jar.

7. Store chutneys in a cool, dark, dry place and leave to mature for at least 8 weeks before using.

Spring rhubarb relish

Season: May to July

Made with the reddish-green stalks of maincrop or 'field' rhubarb, this is quick and easy, involving much less cooking than a chutney would require. It is light, very fruity, and not too sweet. Delicious with curries, oily fish, chicken, cheese and in sandwiches, you'll find it's a versatile addition to the larder.

Rhubarb, by the way, is very easy to prepare but do take care to always remove the leaves as they are poisonous.

Makes 4 x 340g jars
500g granulated sugar
100ml cider vinegar
1kg rhubarb (untrimmed weight)
125g raisins

For the spice bag
50g fresh root ginger, bruised
2 cinnamon sticks, snapped in half
6 cloves

First make your spice bag by tying up the bruised ginger, cinnamon sticks and cloves in a 20cm square of muslin.

Put the sugar, vinegar, 100ml water and the spice bag into a preserving pan. Heat gently to dissolve the sugar and allow the spices to release their flavours into the syrup. Remove from the heat and set aside to infuse for about 20 minutes.

Meanwhile, trim and wipe the rhubarb stalks and chop into 2–2.5cm chunks.

Add the rhubarb and raisins to the spiced syrup. Cook gently for 15–20 minutes until the mixture is thick, but the rhubarb is still discernible as soft chunks. Remove from the heat, pour into warm, sterilised jars (see p.29) and seal with vinegar-proof lids. Use within 12 months.

P.S. To bruise the root ginger for the spice bag, simply whack it gently with a rolling pin or similar blunt object.

Variation

Gooseberries will stand in quite readily for the rhubarb in this recipe. For the spice bag try using a mix of traditional Indian spices: 1 tsp mustard seeds and ½ tsp each of fennel, cumin, nigella and fenugreek seeds.

Chilli pepper jelly

Season: late summer to autumn

The beauty of this recipe is that it is so very simple. Moreover, you can turn up the heat or cool it down to suit your mood by the variety of the chilli pepper you use. Increasingly, these fiery fleshy fruits are being produced by specialist growers in this country (see the directory, p.210). Look out in the late summer and autumn for hot fruity Habanero, rich mild Poblano, tiny hot Thai chillies or flaming Jalapeños to use in this sizzling jelly relish. I like to use red bell peppers, as they are symbolic of the heat, but of course there's no reason why you can't use yellow, orange or green, or a mixture of all four.

Use this punchy jelly relish with cream cheese, smoked mackerel, rice dishes and crispy stir-fried veg.

Makes 4 x 340g jars
750g red bell peppers
100g Jalapeño or other chillies
50g fresh root ginger, peeled
350ml cider vinegar

1kg sugar with added pectin
50ml lime juice (1–2 limes)
1 level tsp salt

Start by slicing both peppers and chillies in half lengthwise and removing the fibrous tissue and countless seeds. Finely chop the peppers, chillies and root ginger or blitz them in a food processor. Place in a large pan, add the vinegar and slowly bring to simmering point. Add the sugar, lime juice and salt, stirring until the sugar has dissolved and the mixture begins to boil.

Boil for 4–6 minutes and then remove from the heat. Allow to cool for 5 minutes, then pour into clean, sterilised jars (see p.29) and seal with vinegar-proof lids. Use within 12 months.

P.S. If you find the pepper pieces rise to the top of the jar as you pot the jelly, leave until the jars are at room temperature, then give them a quick twist – the pepper pieces will redistribute and remain well suspended in the cooling jelly.

Pickled garlic

Season: May to August

Garlic is the strongest-tasting of the *Allium* family, and the moodiest too. It can change character considerably, depending on how it is treated. Left whole and cooked slowly, it is gentle and soft. Chopped up, it will release a little more of its pungent aroma, while crushed to a paste it attains the strong, sometimes bitter flavour that makes it notorious.

When pickled, it remains crisp to the bite, but the flavour becomes really quite mellow – you can eat the cloves straight from the jar. I like to slice the pickled garlic cloves finely and scatter them over salads, or serve them whole as antipasti, or nestle lots of them around a slowly roasting joint of lamb.

Garlic grows well throughout Britain – not just in the veg patch, but also in containers, tubs and even in flower borders, where it can help ward off invasive greenfly. New season's bulbs, with their soft white or purplish-pink skins, are mild and sweet – and much better for pickling than older, drier-skinned garlic, which can be bitter.

Makes 3 x 225g jars

500g new season's garlic bulbs
1 tsp fennel seeds
About 12 peppercorns (black, white or pink)

4–6 bay leaves
200ml cider vinegar
50g granulated sugar
Good pinch of saffron strands

Bring a large pan of water to the boil. Plunge in the garlic for a mere minute, to help loosen the outer skins. Remove from the water, drain and pat dry.

Have ready three warm, sterilised jars (see p.29). Break the garlic bulbs into individual cloves. Peel each clove and pack them into the jars, dropping in the fennel seeds, peppercorns and bay leaves as you go.

Put the vinegar, sugar and saffron into a pan. Bring to the boil and boil for a couple of minutes. Pour the hot vinegar over the garlic, then seal the jars with vinegar-proof lids. Use within a year.

P.S. There are two main types of garlic, hardneck and softneck. Hardnecks produce a flowering spike – or scape – which is usually snapped off to encourage the plant to put its energy into the bulb. These scapes have a delicate, fresh garlic flavour and can be used chopped up in salads, or to make a green and garlicky pesto.

Pickled Florence fennel

Season: June to early July

Tall, willowy, feathered sweet Florence fennel, with its creamy-white, bulbous bottom, has to be one of the most alluring vegetables to grow in the garden. It's not easy to cultivate in every soil but, if it likes your particular situation, you should be able to grow plenty to use with gay abandon in the summertime, with some left over to preserve for later in the year.

It's only really worth making this pickle if you have a supply of freshly lifted bulbs when they are pale green and tender. All too often, the imported stuff is yellow and coarse. You have to discard much of the outer bulb and it certainly isn't worth the expense or trouble of pickling.

This lovely light pickle is delicious with smoked or oily fish and in winter salads. It nearly always makes an appearance at our Boxing Day lunch.

Makes 3 x 340g jars

Salt
1kg fennel bulbs, trimmed and
thinly sliced, a few feathery
fronds reserved
1 litre cider vinegar
15g peppercorns (black, white or pink)

75g granulated sugar
Grated zest of 1 unwaxed lemon
3 or 4 bay leaves
1 tsp celery or fennel seeds
3–4 tbsp olive, hemp or rapeseed oil

Pour 2–3 litres water into a large pan, salt it well and bring to the boil. Add the sliced fennel and blanch for no more than a minute. Drain in a colander, cool under cold water, then drain and pat dry.

Put the vinegar, peppercorns, sugar, lemon zest, bay leaves and celery or fennel seeds into a saucepan. Bring to the boil and continue to boil for about 10 minutes until the liquor reaches a syrupy consistency. The vinegar vapours will create quite a pungent atmosphere in the kitchen.

Pack the fennel into wide-necked, sterilised jars (see p.29), lacing a few fennel fronds between the slices. Remove the vinegar syrup from the heat and carefully pour over the fennel. You may well find all the spices remain at the bottom of the pan. If this happens, distribute them between the jars, poking the peppercorns and bay leaves down through the fennel slices. Pour sufficient oil into each jar to seal the surface. Seal the jars with vinegar-proof lids. Use within 12 months.

Roasted sweet beet relish

Season: June to August

I love the sweet, earthy flavour of beetroot and I hate to see it swamped in strong-tasting vinegar, as so often happens. This light preserve is quite a different proposition: roasting the young roots really concentrates their robust flavour, while the sharp pungency of horseradish adds a liveliness to the sweet beet. Serve this summery relish alongside smoked mackerel. It's also fantastic in sandwiches with cold meats.

Makes 5 x 225g jars

1kg young, small beetroot, trimmed
A little olive oil
250g granulated sugar
150ml red wine vinegar
2 tbsp balsamic vinegar
1 large red onion, peeled and finely chopped

50g freshly grated horseradish root (or pickled horseradish, see below)

For the roasted tomato purée
1kg tomatoes
2 level tsp sea salt
4 garlic cloves, peeled and sliced
50ml olive oil

Preheat the oven to 180°C/Gas Mark 4. For the tomato purée, halve the tomatoes and place them skin side down on a baking tray. Sprinkle with the salt, garlic and olive oil. Roast for an hour or so, on the bottom shelf of the oven, then remove. Rub through a sieve, or pass through a mouli or food mill, to remove the skins and pips – you'll end up with about 300ml of intensely flavoured purée.

Meanwhile, put the beetroot into a baking dish and trickle with a little oil. Roast, above the tomatoes, for 1–1½ hours (longer if necessary) until the skins are blistered, blackened and loosened. Leave to cool a little before peeling. You'll find the skins will slide off easily. Coarsely grate the beetroot (a food processor makes this job easy).

Put the sugar, vinegars, onion and horseradish into a large saucepan, bring to the boil and cook for 5 minutes. Stir in the tomato purée and cook for a couple more minutes. Finally, add the grated beetroot and cook for about 10 minutes, until thickened. Transfer to sterilised jars (see p.29) and seal with vinegar-proof lids. Use within a year. Refrigerate once opened.

P.S. It's easy to pickle horseradish root. Just grate enough freshly dug root to fill a jam jar, sprinkle over 1 tsp salt and 1 tsp sugar, top up with cider vinegar and seal with a lid. Use in sauces, dressings and soups – and, of course, serve with roast beef.

Seasonal chutney

Season: any time from June to October

This is essentially Hugh F-W's classic Glutney, or River Cottage chutney, which first appeared in *The River Cottage Cookbook*. I have not been able to find a better basic chutney recipe. I love it because the flavour is so well balanced (neither too sweet nor too vinegary) and because it is so versatile – allowing you to use whatever gluttish fruit and veg you have to hand, as long as you stick with a similar ratio of fruit/veg to sugar and vinegar. I've included several seasonal variations here.

The fruit and veg chopping is reasonably time-consuming, but important. Whizzing everything up in a food processor would give a very different, sloppy-textured result. From start to finish, the chutney takes about 4 hours to make.

Makes 10–11 x 340g jars

1kg marrows or overgrown courgettes, peeled (if using marrows) and diced

1kg green tomatoes or tomatilloes, peeled and diced

500g cooking apples, peeled, cored and diced

500g onions, peeled and diced

500g sultanas

500g light soft brown sugar

600ml cider vinegar or white wine vinegar

2 tsp dried chilli flakes (optional)

Pinch of salt

For the spice bag

50g fresh root ginger, bruised

12 cloves

2 tsp black peppercorns

1 tsp coriander seeds

Make your spice bag by tying up the spices in a 20cm square of muslin. Put this into a preserving pan with all the other ingredients and bring slowly to the boil, stirring occasionally. This will take a while as there will be lots in the pan, but don't hurry it.

Let the mixture simmer, uncovered, for 2½–3 hours – maybe even a bit more. You do not have to hover, hawk-eyed, over the pan, but do keep an eye on it and stir regularly to ensure it doesn't burn. It's ready when it is glossy, thick, rich in colour and well reduced – but with the chunks of fruit and veg still clearly discernible. It is thick enough if, when you draw a wooden spoon through it, the chutney parts to reveal the base of the pan for a few seconds.

Pot the chutney while warm in sterilised jars (see p.29). Pack down with the back of a spoon to remove any air pockets. Seal with vinegar-proof lids. Store in a cool, dark place and leave for a couple of months to mature before using. Use within 2 years.

Variations

For each, use 500g light soft brown sugar, 600ml cider vinegar or white wine vinegar, a pinch of salt and 2 tsp dried chilli flakes (if liked); follow the basic method (left).

Gingered rhubarb and fig (spring)

1.5kg rhubarb, trimmed and chopped
1kg cooking apples, peeled, cored
 and diced
500g onions, peeled and diced
300g dried figs, chopped and soaked
 overnight in the juice of 3 large
 oranges with the grated zest of 2
100g crystallised ginger, chopped

For the spice bag

2 tsp mustard seeds
2 tsp black peppercorns
50g fresh root ginger, bruised

Plum and pear (late summer)

1kg plums, quartered and stoned
750g pears, peeled, cored and diced
750g cooking apples, peeled, cored
 and diced
500g shallots, peeled and diced
250g stoned prunes, roughly chopped

For the spice bag

50g fresh root ginger, bruised
2 tsp mustard seeds
2 tsp black peppercorns

Apricot and date (late summer)

500g unsulphured dried apricots,
 chopped, soaked overnight, drained
1kg marrow or courgettes, diced
500g cooking apples, peeled, cored
 and diced
500g onions, peeled and diced
250g stoned dates, chopped
250g raisins

For the spice bag

50g fresh root ginger, bruised
1 tsp cloves
1 tsp cumin seeds
1 tsp coriander seeds
2 tsp black peppercorns

Pumpkin and quince (early autumn)

1kg peeled, deseeded pumpkin, diced
1kg quince, peeled, cored and diced
500g cooking apples, peeled, cored
 and diced
500g red onions, peeled and diced
500g raisins
50g freshly grated horseradish root

For the spice bag

2 tsp peppercorns
12 cloves
2 cinnamon sticks

Nasturtium 'capers'

Season: late July to September

After the vibrant trumpets of nasturtium flowers fade, you'll find underneath the foliage the knobbly green seed pods of the plant. They have a hot, peppery flavour and, when pickled, develop a taste very similar to that of true capers (the pickled flowerbuds of the Mediterranean *Capparis* plant). Collect the seed pods on a warm, dry day when all the flowers have wilted away. Gather only the green ones (sometimes they are red-blushed) and avoid any that are yellowing, as these will be dull and dry. The pods can also be used fresh to spice up salads, or as an ingredient in piccalilli (see p.114).

These feisty little pickled nasturtium seed pods are great in fish dishes and in herby, garlicky sauces. Try them in tartare sauce, or add to salads, especially with tomatoes. In fact, use them just as you would capers.

Makes 2 x 115g jars

15g salt	Herbs, such as dill or tarragon sprigs,
100g nasturtium seed pods	or bay leaves (optional)
A few peppercorns (optional)	200ml white wine vinegar

Make a light brine by dissolving the salt in 300ml water. Put the nasturtium seed pods into a bowl and cover with the cold brine. Leave for 24 hours.

Drain the seed pods and dry well. Pack them into small, sterilised jars (see p.29) with, if you like, a few peppercorns and herbs of your choice. Leave room for 1cm of vinegar at the top. Cover the pods with vinegar and seal the jars with vinegar-proof lids. Store in a cool, dark place and leave for a few weeks before eating. Use within a year.

P.S. To make nasturtium tartare sauce, simply mix 100g mayonnaise with 2–3 finely chopped spring onions or 30g finely chopped white part of a leek, 1 tbsp coarsely chopped nasturtium capers, 1 heaped tbsp finely chopped parsley, a squeeze of lemon juice, and salt and pepper to taste. Serve the sauce with simple grilled or fried white fish, hot or cold salmon or trout, or a salad of freshly cooked baby beetroot, young broad beans and rocket or other leaves.

Sweet cucumber pickle

Season: July to September

This is a wonderful way to use up an abundance of cucumbers, be they long and uniform green, or the short, knobbly-skinned ridge type. It's also very quick and easy to make if you use a food processor. This is not a true preserve, as the cucumbers are not brined and the pickle is very light, but it will keep well in the fridge for a couple of weeks in a sealed container.

I love this sweet condiment with all manner of salads, and in sandwiches, but it's especially delectable with hot-smoked trout or salmon.

Makes 2 x 450g jars

1kg cucumbers
3 small onions, red or white
1 tbsp chopped dill (optional)

250g granulated sugar
1 level tbsp salt
200ml cider vinegar

Using the slicing blade of a food processor or a very sharp knife, very finely slice the cucumbers. Peel the onions and slice them very thinly too. Combine the cucumber, onion and dill, if using, in a large bowl.

Mix the sugar, salt and vinegar and pour over the cucumber and onion. Leave overnight for the sweet and sour flavours to mix and mingle or, if this isn't possible, leave for at least 3 hours before serving. Pack into a large airtight container or wide-necked jam jars. Store in the fridge and use within 2 weeks.

Variation

Creamy-white English winter celery makes a lovely sweet pickle, or you can use the more common green celery. Follow the recipe above, replacing the cucumber with 1kg celery. Run a potato peeler lightly down the stalks to remove any tough ribs, then cut into 6–7cm sticks (for crudités or dips) or chop into 1–2cm chunks. Use sweet, mild red onions and season the pickle with celery salt and 1 tsp caraway seeds. As celery does not contain as much water as cucumber, add 200ml water to the vinegar and sugar mixture.

Piccalilli

This traditional sweet vegetable pickle, Indian in origin, is the ultimate August preserve for me. The time to make it is when garden produce is at its peak and there is ample to spare. You can use almost any vegetable in the mix but make sure you include plenty of things which are green and crisp. The secret of a really successful piccalilli is to use very fresh vegetables and to take the time to cut them into small, similar-sized pieces.

The recipe first treats the vegetables to a dry-brining, which helps to keep them really firm and crunchy, then bathes them in a smooth, hot mustard sauce.

Makes 3 x 340g jars

1kg washed, peeled vegetables –
   select 5 or 6 from the following:
   cauliflower or romanesco
   cauliflower; green beans;
   cucumbers; courgettes; green or
   yellow tomatoes; tomatilloes;
   carrots; small silver-skinned
   onions or shallots; peppers;
   nasturtium seed pods
50g fine salt

30g cornflour
10g ground turmeric
10g English mustard powder
15g yellow mustard seeds
1 tsp crushed cumin seeds
1 tsp crushed coriander seeds
600ml cider vinegar
150g granulated sugar
50g honey

Cut the vegetables into small, even bite-sized pieces. Place in a large bowl and sprinkle with the salt. Mix well, cover the bowl with a tea towel and leave in a cool place for 24 hours, then rinse the veg with ice-cold water and drain thoroughly.

Blend the cornflour, turmeric, mustard powder, mustard seeds, cumin and coriander to a smooth paste with a little of the vinegar. Put the rest of the vinegar into a saucepan with the sugar and honey and bring to the boil. Pour a little of the hot vinegar over the blended spice paste, stir well and return to the pan. Bring gently to the boil. Boil for 3–4 minutes to allow the spices to release their flavours into the thickening sauce.

Remove the pan from the heat and carefully fold the well-drained vegetables into the hot, spicy sauce. Pack the pickle into warm, sterilised jars (see p.29) and seal immediately with vinegar-proof lids. Leave (if you can) for 4–6 weeks before opening. Use within a year.

Runner bean pickle

Runner beans are a bit of a love-or-hate vegetable and are often scorned in favour of other green beans. I do sympathise with those that don't eat them – we've all been served rubbery, greying old runners at some time or another and they're no fun at all. However, young tender green runner beans are altogether different and this recipe is just perfect for these guys. It has been eaten and enjoyed by just about everyone who has walked into my kitchen, so I hope that reproducing it here will convert a few more bean-haters.

I see the pickled beans as a preserved vegetable rather than a mere tracklement, and I think they're great alongside cold meats and salads.

Use a couple of jars that are at least 12cm high – taller, if possible – so that the beans can show off their length.

Makes 2 x 450g jars

1kg young runner beans
Salt
300ml cider vinegar or
    white wine vinegar

300g granulated sugar
1 tsp ground allspice
1 tsp coarsely ground black pepper
6 juniper berries (optional)

Start by trimming the ends off the runner beans. If the beans are young and tender, there should be no need to string them. Cut the beans into lengths about 5mm less than the height of the jar you are using.

Bring a pan of lightly salted water to the boil. Add the beans and cook until tender; this should take 5–8 minutes.

Meanwhile, put the vinegar, sugar, 100ml water, allspice, ground pepper and juniper berries, if using, into a pan over a low heat, stirring until the sugar has dissolved. Bring to the boil and boil for a couple of minutes. Drain the runner beans, add them immediately to the spiced vinegar and simmer for 4–5 minutes. Strain the vinegar mixture into a small saucepan.

Pack the beans, upright, into warm, sterilised jars (see p.29); kitchen tongs and a knife are useful for doing this. Return the spiced vinegar to the boil then pour it over the tightly packed beans. Cap immediately with vinegar-proof lids.

Store in a cool, dark place and leave for several weeks to allow the pickle to mature. Use within 12 months.

Sweet pickled damsons

Season: late August to September

Dark-skinned, with a bluish bloom, small oval damsons are very tart and well flavoured, which makes them wonderful for preserving. This is a straightforward recipe that keeps the fruit whole and tender. I love warming cinnamon and allspice in the mix, but you can use any spices you fancy, or even a good tablespoonful of ready-made pickling spice (see p.97). These sweet spiced damsons are a lovely addition to any buffet table and splendid with cold poultry.

Makes 4 x 450g jars
600ml cider vinegar
5cm piece cinnamon stick
1 tsp allspice berries

Finely grated zest and juice of 1 orange
1kg firm, ripe damsons
750g granulated sugar

Put the vinegar, cinnamon, allspice berries, orange zest and juice into a pan and bring to the boil. Boil for 4–5 minutes then strain and allow to cool.

Prick each damson with a needle or skewer (this will prevent them splitting). Add the fruit to the cold spiced vinegar in a clean pan. Bring slowly to simmering point, then simmer very, very gently for 10–15 minutes until the damsons are just tender. Using a slotted spoon, lift out the damsons and pack them into warm, sterilised jars (see p.29).

Return the spiced vinegar to the heat, add the sugar and stir until dissolved. Boil for several minutes to reduce and thicken. Pour this hot spiced syrup over the damsons and seal immediately with vinegar-proof lids. Store in a cool, dark place. These pickled damsons are best kept for 6–8 weeks before eating.

Variations

You can use the same method to pickle firm green gooseberries or cherries. Rhubarb, cut into 5cm chunks, can also be dealt with in this way – but add the sugar with the rhubarb as it will help keep it whole.

Spiced pickled pears

Season: August to December

I love pickled fruits and always look forward to opening a jar to serve with cold poultry and ham. Small, hard pears such as 'Conference' are ideal for use in this recipe, and it's a very good way to deal with a barrel-load of them. If you stick with the basic quantities of sugar and vinegar, this recipe can easily be adapted for use with other fruits and different spices (see the variations below).

Makes 2 x 680g jars

300ml cider vinegar or
    white wine vinegar
400g granulated sugar
25g fresh root ginger, bruised

5cm piece cinnamon stick
1 tsp allspice berries
1kg small, firm pears
1 tsp cloves

Put the vinegar, sugar, ginger, cinnamon and allspice berries into a large pan over a low heat, stirring until the sugar has dissolved, then bring to the boil. Turn down the heat to a simmer.

Meanwhile, start peeling the pears, keeping them whole and with stalks attached. Stud each pear with 2 or 3 cloves and add to the hot vinegar. Simmer the pears very gently until they are tender but not too soft. Remove with a slotted spoon and pack them into warm, sterilised jars (see p.29).

Bring the spiced vinegar syrup to the boil and boil for 5 minutes, then strain it over the pears. Cover the jars with vinegar-proof lids. Keep for at least a month before using. Consume within a year.

Variations

Different spices can be used – try cardamom and coriander, with a flake or two of dried chilli.

Pickled peaches Plunge 1kg peaches into a pan of boiling water for 1 minute, then remove. Immerse them in cold water briefly, then peel. Proceed as for the pear recipe, but simmer the peaches for only 3–4 minutes.

Pickled crab apples Prick 1kg crab apples all over with a needle or skewer (this will prevent the skins bursting). Use well-coloured ornamental varieties such as 'Harry Baker', 'John Downie' or 'Pink Glow'.

Pickled onions

Season: September to November

A good pickled onion is perhaps the doyen of the preserves cupboard – but how do you like yours? Crisp or soft, sweet or sour, mildly spiced or chilli hot? The beauty of this recipe is that it can be used to make your onions (or shallots) just the way you like them. I like mine sweet, so use honey in this recipe, but you could dispense with honey or sugar altogether if you like a really sharp pickle. I also go for cider vinegar, rather than the more traditional malt, because the flavour is less aggressive. The blend of spices used here suits me nicely, but you could also use coriander, cumin or celery seeds – or any other spice you fancy. If you want crisp onions, use cold vinegar; if you like them soft, heat the vinegar first.

Makes 1 x 900g jar

1kg small pickling onions	2–3 mace blades
50g fine salt	2 tsp mustard seeds
600ml vinegar (cider, malt or wine)	1 tsp black or white peppercorns
150g honey or sugar	1 cinnamon stick
15g fresh root ginger, lightly bruised	2 dried chillies (optional)
2 tsp allspice berries	2 bay leaves

Using scissors, snip the top and the rooty bottom off the onions. Place in a large bowl and cover with boiling water. Count steadily to 20 (no more). Drain the onions and plunge into cold water. You will then find the skins will peel off easily.

Put the peeled onions into a shallow dish. Sprinkle with the salt, cover and leave overnight. Meanwhile, pour the vinegar into a pan and add the honey or sugar, ginger and spices (not the bay leaves). Cover and bring to boiling point. Remove from the heat and leave to infuse overnight.

Strain the spiced vinegar. Rinse the onions in very cold water, then drain and pack into a sterilised jar (see p.29), adding the bay leaves as you go. Pour over the vinegar (reheating it first, if you want softer onions) and seal with a vinegar-proof lid. Mature for 6–8 weeks before using. Use within 12 months.

Variation

Use shallots instead of onions and 300ml each red wine vinegar and white wine vinegar. Prepare as above, then pack the shallots into the jar along with 25g sliced fresh root ginger, 1 tsp coriander seeds and a couple of fresh mint sprigs.

Hearty ale chutney

Season: October to January

Spices, onions and a traditional malty ale give this robust, pub-style chutney plenty of character, while the natural sugars in the root veg help sweeten it. It is delicious served with farmhouse Cheddar, crusty bread and a pint or two.

Makes 4–5 x 340g jars

400g onions, peeled and finely sliced

250g swede, peeled and chopped
    into 5mm pieces

200g carrots, peeled and chopped into
    5mm pieces

250g apples, peeled, cored and
    chopped into 1cm pieces

150g cauliflower, broken into
    tiny florets

2 fat garlic cloves, peeled and crushed

100g stoned dates, finely chopped

150g tomato purée

300g demerara sugar

50g dark muscovado sugar

250ml malt or cider vinegar

2 heaped tbsp English mustard powder

2 heaped tsp ground ginger

1 heaped tsp ground mace

1 heaped tsp salt

½ tsp freshly ground black pepper

500ml traditional ale, bitter or stout
    (not lager)

Put all the ingredients, except the ale, into a large pan with 500ml water. Mix well, then place over a low heat and bring to a gentle simmer, stirring until the sugar has dissolved. Cook for about an hour – the vegetables will begin to soften and the juices will thicken and reduce.

Take the pan off the heat and add half the ale. Return to the heat and continue to cook for 30 minutes, by which time the mixture should be deep red-brown in colour. Add the remaining ale and cook for a further 30 minutes. By now the vegetables should be tender, but still retain their shape and a bit of crunch.

Remove from the heat and spoon into warm, sterilised jars (see p.29), making sure there are no air pockets. Seal with vinegar-proof lids. Store for 4–6 weeks before opening. Use within 2 years.

Figgy mostardo

Season: autumn to winter

The Italians use fiery-hot mustard oil to add a bit of passion to their classic fruit preserve *mostardo di cremona*. However, mustard oil is pretty well impossible to purchase in this country, so I have used mustard seeds and powder to pep up the dried figs in my own interpretation of the dish. Serve it with hot or cold meat, oily fish dishes, or with cheese in sandwiches.

Makes 4 x 225g jars

500g dried figs
Finely grated zest and juice of
   2 large grapefruit
1 good tbsp yellow mustard seeds

200g granulated sugar or honey
25g English mustard powder
100ml cider vinegar or white wine
   vinegar

Cut each fig into 4 or 6 pieces – it's easiest to do this using scissors. Place the figs in a bowl and add the grapefruit zest and mustard seeds. Measure the grapefruit juice and make it up to 500ml with water. Pour over the figs. Cover and leave overnight.

Put the figs and juice into a heavy-based saucepan. Heat gently until simmering then add the sugar or honey. Stir until dissolved.

Meanwhile, blend the mustard powder with the vinegar, add to the simmering figs and stir well. Simmer, uncovered, for 20 minutes, stirring occasionally, to reduce and thicken.

Remove the pan from the heat. Spoon the *mostardo* into warm, sterilised jars (see p.29) and seal with vinegar-proof lids. Store for 4 weeks before opening. Use within 12 months.

Variations

Dried apricots, apples or pears, or a good mix of them all, can be used in place of figs. For a stronger, hotter *mostardo*, use black mustard seeds instead of the milder yellow seeds. Orange, lemon or lime juice can replace the grapefruit juice. So you see, you can really make this recipe your very own …

Onion marmalade

Onions are one of the most versatile ingredients in the culinary world, but not often given the chance to be the star of their own show. A recipe like this puts that right. Long, slow cooking turns a panful of red, white or yellow onions into a fantastic rich sauce-cum-jam that's brilliant served with bangers and mash and a heap of other dishes too. Try it with cheese on toast, with cold meat in sandwiches, or stir a spoonful into a creamy pumpkin soup.

Makes 5 x 225g jars

100ml olive oil
2kg onions, peeled and finely sliced
200g demerara sugar
150g redcurrant jelly

300ml cider vinegar
50ml balsamic vinegar
1 rounded tsp salt
½ tsp freshly ground black pepper

Heat the oil in a large pan over a medium heat and add the onions. Reduce the heat, cover the pan and cook over a low heat, stirring occasionally, for 30–40 minutes or until the onions are collapsed and beginning to colour.

Add the sugar and redcurrant jelly. Increase the heat and continue to cook, stirring more frequently, for about 30 minutes until the mixture turns a dark, nutty brown and most of the moisture has been driven off.

Take off the heat and allow to cool for a couple of minutes before adding the vinegars (if you add vinegar to a red-hot pan, it will evaporate in a fury of scorching steam). Return to the heat and cook rapidly for another 10 minutes or so, until the mixture becomes gooey and a spoon drawn across the bottom of the pan leaves a clear track across the base for a couple of seconds.

Remove from the heat and season with the salt and pepper. Spoon into warm, sterilised jars (see p.29) and seal with vinegar-proof lids. Use within 12 months.

P.S. Customarily made from citrus fruit, this marmalade is the exception to the rule. It takes its name and origins from the French, where historically the name 'marmalade' was used to describe fruit that was cooked for a very long time until it was reduced to a thick purée.

Preserved lemons

Season: November to March

Preserved lemons have a strong association with Middle Eastern and North African cuisines and their unique zesty, salty yet mellow flavour permeates many of the traditional meat and couscous dishes. Strips of preserved lemon can also be added to salads, soups and dressings, or mixed with olives and other appetisers. They are exceptionally easy to prepare and I like to make them around the turn of the year when the new season's lemons from Spain and Italy are in the shops.

Makes 2 x 450g jars
1kg small, ripe, unwaxed lemons
150g good-quality sea salt
1 tsp black or pink peppercorns

3–4 bay leaves
1 tsp coriander seeds (optional)

Wash the lemons in cold water and pat them dry. Set 3 or 4 of them aside – these will be squeezed and their juice poured over the salted lemons.

Using a sharp knife, partially quarter the remaining lemons lengthwise by making two deep cuts right through the fruit, keeping them intact at either end. Rub a good teaspoonful of salt into the cut surfaces of each lemon. Pack the fruit chock-a-block into sterilised, wide-necked jars (see p.29), sprinkling in the remaining salt, the peppercorns, bay leaves and coriander seeds as you go.

Squeeze the juice from the reserved lemons and pour over the salted lemons. They must be completely covered. You can top up the jars with a little water if necessary. Seal with a vinegar-proof lid. Leave for at least 4 weeks before opening to allow the lemon rinds to soften.

To use the lemons, remove one from the jar and rinse it well. Scoop out and discard the flesh (or purée it for use in dressings) and use the salted rind whole, chopped or sliced. Make sure the lemons in the jar remain covered with liquid and, once open, keep the jar in the fridge. Use within 12 months.

Cordials, Fruit
Liqueurs & Vinegars

Preserving the essences

of fruits, flowers and herbs by steeping them in alcohol, vinegar or a sugar syrup is the core of these recipes. You might find yourself getting a bit bottled up in this chapter, but don't worry, you'll find it very refreshing and in parts quite intoxicating. Many of the techniques are age-old but are also enjoying a bit of a revival these days – fruit vinegars, in particular, are becoming increasingly popular.

Let me take you on a quick tour of the delicious liquors and infusions:

Cordials, syrups and squashes Essentially these are all concentrated fruity syrups. They are made from strained fruit juice, sweetened with sugar. Some herbs and flowers, such as elderflower, can also be used in a similar way. These smooth infusions can be diluted to taste (usually one part syrup to four or five parts water) to make delicious still or fizzy drinks, or added slowly (to prevent curdling) to ice-cold milk or yoghurt to create shakes and smoothies. Diluted half and half with water and frozen in suitable moulds, they make delicious ice pops. They can also be drizzled neat over ice cream for a quick and easy pudding.

Flavoured vinegars These are very simply made by steeping fruits, herbs or spices in vinegar. The vinegar is then strained (and the flavouring discarded) and usually sweetened. Flavoured vinegars can be used in dressings and mayonnaises, sauces, relishes, pickles and chutneys. They can be trickled neat over a salad, grilled cheese or avocado; diluted with ice-cold water to make a refreshing summer drink (these can be very good); or sipped in the winter to soothe sore, tickly throats. Fruit vinegars are usually made from soft fruits such as raspberries, strawberries or blackberries, which give up their juices easily.

Fruit liqueurs If immersed in alcohol and left in a warm place for several weeks, hedgerow berries, fruit, scented leaves and herbs will give up their flavours beautifully. Sugar is often added to the mix too, during or after steeping, to enhance the flavour. These tipples are not cheap to make but I really value them for their full, smooth flavours, and find a small sup can spirit away annoying thoughts.

Whole fruits in alcohol Raw or lightly cooked fruits can be preserved simply by being sprinkled with sugar and submerging in alcohol. Such fruits make a very special dessert, either on their own or served with a good vanilla ice cream. Be assured that any liquor left after the fruit has been eaten is unlikely to go to waste…

Key ingredients

You'll be amazed at how easily good fresh produce and simple store cupboard ingredients can be transformed into such wide-ranging and stimulating liquors.

Vinegar

Always use a good-quality vinegar with at least 5 per cent acetic acid. Light and fruity cider or wine vinegars are best for flavouring. Use the vinegar cold if it's to be steeped with soft, fresh leaves and flowers, but heat it for the best results with firm ingredients such as garlic, chillies and horseradish. For more on vinegars, see p.37.

Sugar

Refined white or light golden sugars are best in these recipes, to allow the flavours of the fruit, flowers or herbs to prevail. For more information on sugars, see p.35.

Alcohol

This is a very effective preserving medium, but needs to be in the form of spirit with at least 40 per cent alcohol (80 per cent proof). See p.38 for more information.

Fruit

This must be fresh, of the highest quality and definitely not under-ripe. In fact, fruit that is a little too ripe for jam, or for bottling, is ideal for fruit syrups. Perfectly ripe fruit should be used for preserved whole fruits and fruit liqueurs – prick it with a needle or skewer in several places to help the juices flow. Only wash the fruit if absolutely necessary. Otherwise prepare as follows:

Strawberries and raspberries Remove the hull
Cherries Stone or not, it's up to you
Peaches and apricots Peel if you like, then slice or quarter
Plums and damsons Halve or leave whole. If leaving whole, prick with a fork or skewer
Pears Peel or not, then core, halve or quarter
Grapes Remove the stems
Early blackberries Pick over

Herbs, spices and flowers

It is important to gather herbs and flowers when they are fully dry and ideally when they have been gently warmed by the sun. This is when their characteristic oils and essences are at their best and most pungent. Likewise, spices and aromatics should be fresh and strong-smelling.

Shelf life and keepability

Fruit vinegars and liqueurs are best used within 2 years, although providing they are well sealed and kept in a cool, dry place, they will keep for considerably longer. Fruit syrups, cordials and squashes have a shorter shelf life – they can be kept in a cool, dry place, or the refrigerator, for a few weeks, or frozen. You can, however, extend their shelf life as follows:

Extending shelf life of fruit syrups, cordials and squashes to 4 months
Sterilise your bottles and their corks, swing-top lids or screw-tops by putting them all in a large pan of water and bringing to the boil. Leave them in the pan so they are still hot when you are ready to use them.

Bring the fruit syrup or squash to just above simmering point (check it reaches 88–90°C on a sugar thermometer). Using a funnel, fill the hot bottles to within 1cm of the brim if you're using screw-tops or swing-stoppers, or within 2.5cm of the brim if you're using corks. Fill each bottle and seal it before filling the next bottle. This method avoids using a deep-pan hot water bath (it is well-nigh impossible to find a pan deep enough to fully submerge bottles).

Extending shelf life of fruit syrups, cordials and squashes to 1 year To do this, you need to process the filled bottles in a hot water bath (see p.164). Fill the bottles with syrup to within 2.5cm of the tops for screw-tops or swing-stopper lids, and to within 3.5cm of the tops if you are using corks – this allows for expansion and prevents the tops blowing off. Screw-lids should be put on lightly and then tightened when the bottles are taken out of the water bath. Corks need to be held down and prevented from blowing off during the heating process by securing them with some strong insulation tape. Swing-tops should be fully sealed – the rubber ring will allow steam to escape.

Stand the filled, sealed bottles in a deep pan on a trivet or folded tea towel. Fill the pan with water, to within 2.5cm of the top of the bottles, and bring to simmering point (88°C). Keep at this temperature for 20 minutes. Remove from the pan and leave to cool.

Once cold, bottles that have been sealed with a cork can be made airtight by dipping the cork and the top 1cm of the bottle into melted paraffin wax or beeswax.

Storage after opening Whichever method you choose, once opened the bottles should be kept in the fridge.

Family 'beena

Season: pretty much all year round

I'd like to introduce you to a group of cordials with a name inspired by a certain well-known fruit squash. These can be prepared throughout the year and are an excellent way of using fruit that's too ripe for jam-making. I've made rhubeena with rhubarb, berrybeena with summer berries, plumbeena with plums and dambeena with damsons – and currants, of course, work very well too. Use these fruits alone to make single variety 'beenas or, for a lighter and more economical cordial, use 50 per cent cooking apples.

Because the fruit pulp will be strained, you needn't be too fastidious with its preparation. Rhubarb should be cut into chunks. Strawberries should be hulled. Plums are best halved, but it's not necessary to remove the stones. Apples should be de-stalked and roughly chopped, but there's no need to peel or core them.

Makes about 1.5 litres
2kg fruit
Granulated sugar
Brandy (optional)

Place your chosen prepared fruit in a large saucepan. For each 1kg blackcurrants, apples or hard fruit, add 600ml water; for each 1kg plums or stone fruit, add 300ml water; for each 1kg soft berries or rhubarb, add 100ml water. Bring slowly to the boil, crushing the fruit with a wooden spoon or potato masher, and cook gently until the fruit is soft and the juices flowing. This will take anything up to 45 minutes depending on the type of fruit. Remove from the heat.

Scald a jelly bag or fine tea towel (see p.41) and suspend over a large bowl. Tip the fruit into it and leave to drip overnight.

Measure the resulting juice and pour into a clean pan. For every 1 litre juice, add 700g sugar (or to taste). Heat the mixture gently to dissolve the sugar, then remove from the heat. Pour immediately into warm, sterilised bottles (see p.133), leaving a 1cm gap at the top. At this point you may like to add a couple of teaspoonfuls of brandy to each bottle. Seal with a screw-top or cork.

'Beenas will keep for several months, provided they are sealed when hot and stored in a cool place. However, if you want to keep them for longer you will need to sterilise the bottles in a water bath immediately after bottling (see p.133).

Lemon squash

Season: November to March

A cool glass of this home-made squash knocks the commercially produced alternative into oblivion. Once tasted, this will become a favourite thirst-quencher. Serve diluted with cold water as a cool summertime refresher, or mix with tonic water and a splash of Angostura bitters for a non-alcoholic cocktail. You can also ring the changes and use oranges as well as lemons for a St Clement's squash.

Makes 2–3 x 500ml bottles
7–10 unwaxed lemons
650g granulated sugar

Scrub the lemons and pare the zest from four of them. Bring a pan of water to the boil, drop in the lemons and leave for 1 minute. Lemons are often quite hard and unyielding – this will soften them and they will give more juice when squeezed. Lift out the lemons and keep the lemon-infused water to one side. Squeeze the juice from the lemons and measure out 500ml of it.

Put the sugar, lemon zest and 500ml of the lemony water into a saucepan. Heat gently to dissolve the sugar, then bring to the boil. Add the 500ml lemon juice and bring just to boiling point. Remove from the heat and strain through a sieve into a jug. Pour immediately into hot, sterilised bottles (see p.133) and seal immediately with sterilised screw-caps, corks or swing-top lids.

Leave to cool, then store the squash in a cool, dry place or the fridge for up to 4 months. For longer keeping – up to a year – sterilise the bottles in a water bath (as directed on p.133).

To serve the squash, mix one part syrup to four parts water.

P.S. Another way to increase the yield of juice from citrus fruits is to roll the fruit back and forth over a work surface, pressing down firmly with the palm of your hand, for 2–3 minutes.

Beech leaf noyau

Season: late April to early May

The name for this unusual alcoholic cordial is actually the French word for 'fruit stone'. Traditionally, it was made from bitter almonds or peach stones mixed with gin, then left to steep in a warm place for several days before being cooked up with sugar then filtered through blotting paper. This recipe is from Richard Mabey's excellent *Food for Free*. It uses the young, silken leaves of our native beech tree (*Fagus sylvatica*), which first appear towards the end of April, to make an exquisite hedgerow version of the liqueur.

Makes 1 litre

1 loosely packed carrier bagful
   of soft young beech leaves
500ml gin

300g granulated sugar
Brandy

Pack the beech leaves into an earthenware or glass jar until it's about nine-tenths full. Pour the gin over the leaves, making sure they are well covered (they will oxidise and turn brown if left exposed). Leave to steep for 7–10 days so the leaves can release their striking green pigment. Strain the infused gin through muslin or a jelly bag (see p.41).

Put the sugar and 250ml water into a saucepan and heat gently to dissolve the sugar. Allow to cool completely before adding to the infused gin. Add a couple of capfuls of brandy too.

Put a couple of fresh beech leaves into a sterilised screw-top or stopper bottle (see p.133), then add the noyau and seal.

Wait for a cold winter night and a roaring fire, then partake of this potent liqueur. Use within 2 years (it may darken in colour over time).

P.S. If you miss the young beech leaves of early spring, you may get a second chance to make this noyau towards the end of June. Some beech hedges, when trimmed, will throw up new young shoots – not as prolific as the early crop, but still worth snatching.

Elderflower cordial

Season: late May to June

The sweetly scented, creamy-white flowers of the elder tree appear in abundance in hedgerows, scrub, woodlands and wasteland at the beginning of summer. The fresh flowers make a terrific aromatic cordial. They are best gathered just as the many tiny buds are beginning to open, and some are still closed. Gather on a warm, dry day (never when wet), checking the perfume is fresh and pleasing. Trees do differ and you will soon get to know the good ones. Remember to leave some flowers for elderberry picking later in the year.

This recipe is based on one from the River Cottage archives: it's sharp, lemony and makes a truly thirst-quenching drink. You can, however, adjust it to your liking by adding more or less sugar. The cordial will keep for several weeks as is. If you want to keep it for longer, either add some citric acid and sterilise the bottles after filling (see p.133), or pour into plastic bottles and store in the freezer.

Serve the cordial, diluted with ice-cold sparkling or still water, as a summer refresher – or mix with sparkling wine or Champagne for a classy do. Add a splash or two, undiluted, to fruit salads or anything with gooseberries – or dilute one part cordial to two parts water for fragrant ice lollies.

Makes about 2 litres

About 25 elderflower heads

Finely grated zest of 3 unwaxed lemons and 1 orange, plus their juice (about 150ml in total)

1kg sugar

1 heaped tsp citric acid (optional) (see the directory, p.210)

Inspect the elderflower heads carefully and remove any insects. Place the flower heads in a large bowl together with the orange and lemon zest. Bring 1.5 litres water to the boil and pour over the elderflowers and citrus zest. Cover and leave overnight to infuse.

Strain the liquid through a scalded jelly bag or piece of muslin (see p.41) and pour into a saucepan. Add the sugar, the lemon and orange juice and the citric acid (if using). Heat gently to dissolve the sugar, then bring to a simmer and cook for a couple of minutes.

Use a funnel to pour the hot syrup into sterilised bottles (see p.133). Seal the bottles with swing-top lids, sterilised screw-tops or corks.

Elixir of sage

Season: spring and summer

The healing, warming properties of sage have long been recognised and one traditional way to imbibe them is by means of a liqueur, such as this one. The velvety, grey-green leaves are steeped in eau de vie and the resulting elixir should, I'm told, be drunk each day to ensure good health and a long life. I take just a capful (not a cupful) myself each morning and find it very restorative. Of course, this is not the only way to use this soothing herb liqueur – a glassful can be enjoyed as a comforting digestif or a capful diluted with tonic water for an aromatic pick-me-up.

Gather the sage on a warm, dry day. As an evergreen, this herb can be picked throughout the year but it's at its best during the spring and summer months.

Makes 1 litre

50–60g sage leaves (about ¼ of a carrier bagful)

500ml eau de vie
200g granulated sugar

Shake the sage leaves well to remove any wildlife (those that don't escape at this stage will become sublimely intoxicated). Pack the leaves into a large, wide-necked jar, of 600–700ml capacity. Fill the jar to the very top with eau de vie and seal with an airtight lid (if any leaves are uncovered they will oxidise and the colour of the liquor will become dull brown). Give it a good shake and then place on a sunny windowsill to steep for about 30 days, remembering to give it a shake every now and then.

When you're ready to complete the elixir, make a sugar syrup by gently heating the sugar with 200ml water until the sugar has dissolved. Allow this to cool.

Strain the sage liquor through a sieve into a bowl. Mix the strained liquor with the sugar syrup. Decant into clean sterilised bottles (see p.133), placing 2 or 3 of the soaked sage leaves in the bottle. Cork or cap with screw-caps. The elixir will be ready to use immediately. Consume within a year.

Currant shrub

A shrub is an old-fashioned kind of drink: essentially a delightfully fruity, alcoholic cordial. Based on sweetened rum or brandy, it is traditionally flavoured with acidic fruit such as Seville oranges, lemons or redcurrants. Keep back some of the juice after straining redcurrants to make jelly (see recipe, p.62) and you will find this lovely tipple very simple to make.

Serve as an aperitif, either on its own or mixed half and half with dry martini and finished with a splash of fresh orange juice, which is my favourite way.

Makes about 1 litre
300ml strained redcurrant juice
600ml rum or brandy
Finely grated zest of 1 orange

1 tsp grated nutmeg
300g granulated sugar

Mix the redcurrant juice, rum or brandy, orange zest and nutmeg together in a large, wide-necked jar. You may find the mixture of acid and alcohol forms a gel – a perfect example of how adding fruit juice to spirit can determine pectin levels (see pp.46–7). Don't worry, the mixture will become liquid again when you add the sugar. Seal the jar tightly and leave for 7–10 days in a cool, dark place.

Transfer the currant and alcohol mixture to a pan, add the sugar and heat gently to about 60°C. When the sugar has dissolved, strain the liqueur through a jelly bag or muslin (see p.41). Decant the strained liquid into a sterilised bottle (see p.133) and seal with a cap.

Store for several months in a cool, dark place so the shrub can fully mature before you take the first tipple. Use within 2 years.

P.S. Redcurrants that grow on a standard (long-stemmed) bush, rather than at ground level, make picking very easy and also add interest to the garden. I pick 4–5kg redcurrants each season from my standard bush.

Variation
At marmalade-making time, buy an extra kilo of Seville oranges and use the strained juice in place of the redcurrant juice for an outstanding orange liqueur.

Mint syrup

Season: June to August

I can't help feeling that we should all make more use of garden mint (*Mentha spicata*). I'm sure that if it didn't run amok in the garden in a rather annoying way, we would prize it more highly not just as a nice thing to chuck in with the potatoes, but as the wonderful sweet-scented herb that it is.

This simple recipe is best made with young, bright green mint leaves, picked just before flowering, when the volatile oils are at their strongest. Gather them on a sunny day, when the plant is fully dry and the leaves are warm. Use the leaves immediately after picking to retain every bit of their amazing warming-and-cooling menthol character.

Mix 10ml mint syrup into a glass of ice-cold water, lemonade or tonic for a cooling summer drink. To make delicious hot, sweet mint tea, add 1 tbsp of the syrup to a pot (silver, of course, if you have one) of steaming green tea.

Makes 1 litre

50g freshly picked mint leaves	250g sugar
Juice of 1 lemon (50ml)	1 level tsp sea salt

Check the mint leaves for any insect life then tear the leaves into shreds. Put the lemon juice into a large bowl. Add the mint and pound with the end of a wooden rolling pin. Add the sugar and the salt and continue to crush the mint leaves to release their menthol essence. Leave to macerate for 8–10 hours or overnight.

Pour 600ml boiling water over the macerated mint mixture and leave to stand for a further 12 hours.

Strain the syrup through a very fine sieve or muslin into a saucepan. Gently bring to simmering point and simmer for a couple of minutes. Pour into warm, sterilised bottles (see p.133) and seal with screw-caps or corks.

This syrup will keep unopened for 4 months, but once opened, it should be stored in the fridge. If you want to keep it longer, it will need to be sterilised in a water bath straight after bottling (see p.133).

Flavoured vinegars

Season: June to November

These are very useful additions to the store cupboard as their distinctive flavours can revolutionise a simple salad dressing or sauce. The process is simple: aromatic herbs, flowers or strong-flavoured ingredients are steeped in vinegar for a period of time and are then strained out. The vinegar is then decanted into a sterilised bottle and sealed (see p.133).

Always pick leaves and flowers for steeping when they are dry and their perfume is at its best. Use cider vinegar or white wine vinegar, rather than the stronger malt – or perhaps try some delicate rice vinegar to give a hint of Asian flavour to the mix.

Horseradish vinegar

Peel and grate 50g freshly dug horseradish root and pack into a large sterilised jar with 2 finely chopped shallots, 1 tsp sugar and ½ tsp salt. Heat 600ml cider vinegar to just below boiling and pour over the mix. Seal and leave for a month or so before straining and bottling. I like to use this vinegar for pickling cucumber or beetroot.

Nasturtium vinegar

Fill a wide-necked jar of 570ml capacity with freshly gathered, brilliantly coloured nasturtium flowers, a few spicy nasturtium seed pods (see p.111), 2 chopped shallots, 8–10 peppercorns and ½ tsp salt. Pour over 500ml cold white wine vinegar. Leave for 30 days or so in a sunny spot, giving the jar a shake every now and then. Strain the vinegar and discard the flowers. Pack into a sterilised jar with a couple of fresh nasturtium flowers to identify the vinegar.

To make a splendid summer salad dressing, add 1 tbsp soy sauce to 100ml nasturtium vinegar and whisk in 200ml olive or rapeseed oil.

Mixed herb vinegar

Mix 4 heaped tbsp herbs – chives, parsley, tarragon, fennel, thyme, or whatever you have – with 500ml cold white wine vinegar or cider vinegar. Leave for 3–4 weeks in a cool, dark place. Strain, discard the herbs and bottle.

Spiced samphire vinegar

Pack 50g samphire, 6 allspice berries and 2 finely chopped shallots into a large jar. Pour over 500ml cold rice vinegar or cider vinegar. Leave for 2–3 months before straining and bottling. This is great for fish dishes, and in sweet and sour sauces.

Raspberry vinegar

Season: July to August

Sweetened vinegars are yet another way to preserve the flavour and character of summertime fruits such as raspberries. Historically, these concoctions were valued for their medicinal qualities, and were typically used to relieve coughs and treat fevers and colds. During the nineteenth century, raspberry vinegar in particular was recommended as a refreshing tonic to overcome weariness. But fruit vinegars have a multitude of culinary uses too and I certainly wouldn't want to be without a bottle or two in the kitchen.

Use raspberry vinegar on salads – either neat, or blended with olive oil. I also love it trickled over goat's cheese, pancakes and even ice cream. You'll also find that a spoonful adds a lovely piquancy to savoury sauces. For a revitalising summer drink, mix a couple of tablespoonfuls of raspberry vinegar with soda or tonic water and add ice.

The fruit for a vinegar needs to be gathered on a dry day. If the fruit is wet, it will dilute the vinegar and adversely affect its keeping quality.

Makes 1.5 litres
1kg raspberries
600ml cider vinegar or
white wine vinegar
Granulated sugar

Put the raspberries in a bowl and crush them lightly with a wooden spoon. Add the vinegar. Cover the bowl and leave the fruit and vinegar to steep for 4–5 days, stirring occasionally.

Pour the fruit and vinegar into a scalded jelly bag or piece of muslin suspended over a bowl (see p.41) and leave to drain overnight. You can squeeze it a little if you like.

Measure the liquid then pour into a saucepan. For every 600ml fruit vinegar, add 450g sugar. Place over a low heat and bring gently to the boil, stirring until the sugar has dissolved. Boil for 8–10 minutes, removing any scum as it rises. Remove from the heat and leave to cool. Bottle and seal when cold. Use within 12 months.

Variations
Replace the raspberries with the same quantity of strawberries, blackcurrants or blackberries to create other fruit vinegars.

Rosehip syrup

Season: late September to October

The shapely rosehip is the fleshy fruit of our native hedgerow rose. The orange-red berries that appear in the autumn contain a crowd of creamy white seeds, protected by tiny irritant hairs, which is why they should never be eaten raw.

Rosehips are rich in vitamins A and C and have long been used for making jams, jellies, wine, tea and, of course, syrup. This recipe is based on one issued by the Ministry of Defence during the Second World War when rosehips were gathered by volunteers. They were paid 3d (just over 1p) for each pound (450g) they collected and the syrup made from the fruit was fed to the nation's children.

Use this rosehip syrup, mixed with hot water, as a warming winter drink. I also love it drizzled neat over rice pudding or pancakes.

Or try this recipe of Hugh F-W's for a refreshing summer cocktail: pour 30ml rosehip syrup into a tall glass. Add 60ml white rum and mix well. Add a few ice cubes and pour over about 150ml tart apple juice. Garnish with a sprig of mint and serve with a straw.

Makes about 1.5 litres
500g rosehips
650g granulated sugar

Pick over the rosehips, removing the stalks, and rinse in cold water.

Put 800ml water in a pan and bring to the boil. Meanwhile, mince the rosehips or chop them in a food processor. Add them to the pan of boiling water, cover and bring back to the boil. Take off the heat and allow to stand for 15 minutes. Pour through a scalded jelly bag or muslin (see p.41) and leave to drip for an hour or so.

Set aside the strained juice. Bring another 800ml water to the boil, add the rosehip pulp, and repeat the boiling process. Tip the mixture back into the jelly bag or muslin and this time leave to drain overnight.

The next day, combine both lots of strained juice (you can discard the rosehip pulp). Measure the juice (you should have about 1 litre) and pour into a saucepan. Add the sugar and heat, stirring until dissolved. Boil for 2–3 minutes, then immediately pour into warm, sterilised bottles (see p.133) and secure with a screw-cap or cork.

Use within 4 months. If you want to keep the syrup for longer, you'll need to sterilise the bottles in a water bath (see p.133).

Sloe gin

Season: September to October

This is undoubtedly the best-known of the hedgerow liqueurs. It is best made with sloes that have been lightly frosted on the first cold nights of the year. (The frost helps to break down the internal structure of the fruit and get the juices flowing.) However, if the first frosts are late in arriving, you might miss the sloes because they'll have been eaten by birds. To avoid this, pick them late in September and pop in the freezer. Alternatively, prick the sloes all over with a skewer.

If you enjoy this hedgerow tipple, try some of my other favourites below. There is no reason why you cannot use vodka instead of gin.

Makes about 1 litre
450g sloes, frosted or pricked (see above)
450g sugar (or less for a more tart gin)
600ml gin

Put the sloes into a large clean jar or bottle. Pour over the sugar, followed by the gin. Secure the container with the lid and give it a good shake to mix up the contents. Shake daily for the next week to prevent the sugar from settling on the bottom and to help release the sloe juice. Thereafter shake and taste once a week for 8–10 weeks.

When the sloes have instilled their flavour, pass the mixture through a fine sieve. Pour the strained liqueur into bottles.

Ideally, you should leave sloe gin for 18 months before drinking, so it pays to have a year's batch in hand. Of course, that's not always possible – but do try and stash a bottle or two away to savour when it's mature and mellow.

And what to do with all those gin-soaked sloes? You can either eat them just as they are, or remove the stones and serve the fruit with ice cream, or fold into melted chocolate to make delectable petits fours.

Variations

In each case, follow the method for sloe gin, but with the following quantities:

Damson gin Use 450g damsons, pricked, 225g sugar and 600ml gin.

Blackberry and apple gin Use 225g blackberries, 225g cooking apples, peeled and chopped, 225g sugar and 600ml gin.

Cherry ratafia Use 500g cherries, pricked, 500ml eau de vie, 2 cinnamon sticks and 150g vanilla sugar.

Haw brandy Use 450g haws, 225g sugar and 600ml brandy.

Bachelor's jam

Season: June to October

This is also known as officer's jam but it's really not a jam at all. The German name, *Rumtopf*, seems far more appropriate for what is actually a cocktail of rum-soaked fruit. The idea is that the mixture of fruit, alcohol and sugar is added to gradually, as different fruits ripen throughout the growing season. This preserve is usually prepared with Christmas in mind, when the potent fruity alcohol is drunk and the highly spirited fruit can be served on its own or with ice cream and puddings. It's not essential to use rum, by the way – brandy, vodka or gin will work just as well.

You will need a large glazed stoneware or earthenware pot with a closely fitting lid, and a small plate, saucer or other flat object that will fit inside the pot and keep the fruit submerged.

Fruit in season (see p.132 for preparation)
1–2 litres rum, brandy, vodka or gin (40 per cent)
Granulated sugar (250g to every 500g fruit)

Choose just-ripe fruits as they appear through the summer and autumn. I normally kick off the pot with some of the first small, sweet strawberries of the season. Place these in the bottom of your pot or jar and, for every 500g fruit, sprinkle over 250g sugar. Leave this for an hour or so then pour over about 1 litre of your chosen alcohol. Place the saucer on top of the fruit to make sure the fruit remains immersed. Then cover the pot with cling film or plastic and, finally, a close-fitting lid.

Carry on like this throughout the summer and autumn, adding raspberries, cherries, peaches, plums, damsons, pears, grapes and blackberries as they come into season. (I avoid currants and gooseberries because their skins tend to toughen in the alcohol syrup, and I find rhubarb is too acid for the pot). Add the sugar each time too, and keep topping up the alcohol so that it always covers the fruit by about 2cm.

Do not stir the fruit at any point, just let it sit in its layers. When the pot is full to the brim, seal it tightly and leave for a couple of months before you start enjoying the contents. Just prior to using, dig deep and give the contents a good stir to combine all the scrumptious flavours. Use within 12 months.

P.S. If you're in a hurry, you can make bachelor's jam in one go in August, when lots of different fruits should be available. However, I do find it more fun to add the fruit over several months, whenever I have a surplus.

Bottled Fruits

With the advent of the deep-freeze, bottling

has rather slipped from necessity and fashion. That's a shame as it is an excellent way of preserving fruits – far better than freezing for some – such as peaches, cherries, figs and apricots. These, when bottled, will remain closer in flavour and texture to their natural state. Another advantage of bottling is that the fruit is ready and waiting to be used at any moment – there's none of that ferreting about in the bottom of the freezer or waiting for a soggy mass of fruit to defrost.

Nevertheless, unravelling the bottling process can seem like cracking a secret code. There are so many methods to choose from – the slow water method, the quick water method, the very low oven, moderate oven or pressure cooker – as well as charts to navigate. To make it easier and to encourage you to have a go, I have whittled down bottling to two basic methods that can be used for most fruits – the water bath method and the oven method. To be successful, both rely on two simple points – the fruit must be sterilised by heating and the jars perfectly sealed.

Jars and bottles

The containers used for bottling are stronger than normal jam jars because they need to withstand a heating process. Two types are generally used (see below) and both are available in 250ml, 500ml, 750ml, 1 litre, 1.5 litre and 2 litre capacities (see the directory, p.210, for suppliers).

The jars, lids and rubber rings should be sterilised before the fruit is packed in. I find the easiest way to do this is to place them in a large pan of cold water and bring slowly to boiling point. I then remove the pan from the heat and leave the jars in the water until I need them. The safest way to remove the jars from the pan is with a pair of tongs. There is no need to dry the jars. Alternatively, before use, the jars can be washed in hot water, left inverted to drain, then put in a cool oven (140°C/Gas Mark 1) for 15 minutes.

Screw-band jars Often referred to as Kilner jars, these have metal or glass lids and are fitted with rubber rings that separate the top of the jar and the lid. The screw-band is fully tightened only after the cooking process, to seal the jar and form a vacuum.

Clip jars Often known as Le Parfait jars, these also have a rubber ring to separate the jar top from the lid but are fastened with a metal spring clip. These jars allow steam to escape, but no air can enter. They normally have a wider mouth than screw-band jars and are therefore more suitable for use with larger fruits such as pears or peaches.

In both cases, the rubber rings must be a perfect fit and in perfect condition – so check them before using. They will deteriorate with use and will need replacing from time to time. The rubber rings can either be sterilised with the jars and lids, or soaked in warm water for 15 minutes (this makes it much easier to stretch them on), then dipped in boiling water just before they go on the jar.

Preparing syrup

Fruit can be bottled in plain water but a syrup based on sugar or honey will improve the flavour. Alcohol, pure fruit juice, fruit cordials, scented leaves and spices can be added to give character and interest. The strength of the syrup depends on the type of fruit used and how you like your fruit to taste – the tarter the fruit, the heavier you'll want to make the syrup. Generally, you want a sweeter syrup for more tightly packed fruit too, because less is used. Syrups are always prepared by simply dissolving the required amount of sugar or honey in water and boiling for 1 minute.

Light syrup 100g sugar, 600ml water
Medium syrup 175g sugar, 600ml water
Heavy syrup 250g sugar, 600ml water

Fruit for bottling

This should ideally be perfectly ripe, but err on the side of under rather than over if you have to. Handle the fruit carefully as any bruising will spoil the preserve. Prepare it by removing stalks, stems, leaves and hulls, and rinsing in cold water if necessary.

Plums, damsons and cherries These can be bottled whole or stoned – stones will impart an agreeable almondy flavour. There's no need to prick the fruit.

Gooseberries These are best bottled when green and slightly under-ripe. The skins should be pricked or nicked to prevent shrivelling.

Pears and apples These should be peeled and cored before bottling. Pears can be cored and quartered or left whole. Once peeled, place in a bowl of salted water (25g salt to 1 litre water) to prevent discoloration until ready to pack.

Peaches, apricots and nectarines These should be peeled: immerse in boiling water for 1 minute then plunge into cold water, peel and pack immediately.

Rhubarb These stalks should be chopped into 2.5–5cm lengths and steeped overnight in a light to medium syrup prior to packing and processing.

Soft fruits Handle these as little as possible – just remove stalks or hulls.

Vegetables These require a very high-temperature process and are not suitable for home bottling by either of the methods covered in this book.

Packing tips

Fruit to be bottled should be handled as little as possible. Packing the fruit in neatly will mean you can get more in the jar.

1. Fruit will shrink during the heating process so should be packed into jars as tightly as possible, but without bruising.

2. Use a long-handled packing spoon, the end of a wooden spoon or a chopstick to position fruit and tease out any air bubbles.

3. Stand jars on a wooden surface or newspaper when filling with hot syrup.

4. Make sure the rim of the jar is free from pips or fruit fibres.

5. Give the jar a sharp knock or twizzle to remove any trapped air before sealing.

The water bath method

For bottling in this way, you need a pan deep enough to contain the jars completely submerged under water. The jars will crack if they sit directly on the base of the pan, so it needs a 'false bottom' such as a wire trivet or a folded tea towel. A thermometer is essential to check the temperature.

The fruit should be packed into jars and filled to the brim with hot syrup (about 60°C). If you're using screw-band jars, the band should be released by a quarter of a turn for steam to escape. Place the jars in the pan and cover completely with warm water (38°C). Heat to simmering point (88°C) over a period of 25–30 minutes, then simmer for the time given in the recipe or the chart (overleaf).

Remove the jars one at a time and place them on a wooden surface, newspaper or folded cloth – scooping out some of the water first will make it much easier to lift the jars from the pan. Tighten the bands on screw-band jars, then leave undisturbed for 24 hours until completely cool. Check the seal the following day (see overleaf).

The oven method

This takes longer than the water bath method but means you can process more jars at a time and you don't need to worry about finding a deep pan.

Preheat the oven to 150°C/Gas Mark 2. Stand the jars about 5cm apart (enough to allow the warm air to circulate) on a thick pad of newspaper, or stand them on newspaper or a folded tea towel in a baking tray filled with water to a depth of 3cm. Fill the packed jars with boiling syrup and cover with the rubber rings and jar tops, but do not fasten with clips or screw-bands at this stage.

Heat in the oven for the time given on the chart (see right). Remove the jars, one at a time, seal with the screw-band or clip immediately and place on a wooden surface, newspaper or folded cloth. Leave undisturbed until completely cool and check the seal the following day (see below).

Testing the seal

It's important to do this after bottling to check that the seal is absolutely airtight. When the jars are completely cool, undo the clips or remove the screw-bands. Put one hand underneath the jar and, with the other hand, carefully lift the jar by the lid. If it's well sealed, the lid will remain firmly on. You can then re-fasten the clip or screw-band and put the jar away for storage. If it comes away, either reprocess the fruit or eat it up immediately.

Storage

Store bottled fruits in a cool, dark and dry place. They will keep well for up to a year. After this, although there may be nothing wrong with them, the texture and colour will begin to deteriorate.

Opening jars

The round rubber seal on a Le Parfait jar has a small protuberance which when pulled should break the seal. However, it doesn't always work! So for awkward Le Parfait jars and Kilner jars, very carefully insert the point of a knife between the rubber ring and the rim and gently lever up. If the seal is still difficult to break, then stand the jar in hot water for a few minutes – this will help to release the seal.

Heating times for water bath and oven bottling methods

For safe bottling it is important to adhere to these timings. For the water bath method, check the water temperature with a thermometer; for the oven method, preheat the oven and check the temperature using an oven thermometer.

FRUIT	WATER BATH METHOD	OVEN METHOD
Apple slices **Blackberries** **Blueberries** **Currants** **Gooseberries** **Loganberries** **Mulberries** **Raspberries** **Strawberries** **Rhubarb**	Maintain at simmering point (88°C) for 2 minutes	30–40 minutes for jars up to 1 litre 45–50 minutes for 1–2 litre jars
Apricots **Cherries** **Damsons** **Greengages** **Plums, whole**	Maintain at simmering point (88°C) for 10 minutes	40–50 minutes for jars up to 1 litre 50–60 minutes for 1–2 litre jars
Nectarines **Peaches** **Plums, halved**	Maintain at simmering point (88°C) for 20 minutes	50–60 minutes for jars up to 1 litre 60–70 minutes for 1–2 litre jars
Figs **Pears** **Tomatoes, whole**	Maintain at simmering point (88°C) for 40 minutes	60–70 minutes for jars up to 1 litre 70–80 minutes for 1–2 litre jars
Fruit purées and pulps (these need to be poured at boiling point into hot jars)	Maintain at simmering point (88°C) for 5 minutes for fruit pulp, 10 minutes for tomato purée	Not applicable

Early rhubarb with honey

Season: January to February

The arrival of the early 'forced' rhubarb in January deserves a salutation of the greatest magnitude and I can never wait to savour its fresh, earthy energy. The blushing stalks, with their tart but delicate flavour, are strictly seasonal, so be sure you don't miss the chance to bottle a jar or two to enjoy later in the year.

Makes 2 x 500ml jars
150g honey
Juice of 1 large orange (you need 100ml)
1.5kg forced rhubarb

Put the honey and 500ml water into a pan and slowly bring to the boil to make a syrup. Remove from the heat and add the orange juice.

Meanwhile, wipe the rhubarb and trim the ends. Cut into even 2.5–5cm chunks. Place the rhubarb in a bowl and pour over the hot syrup. Leave to stand for 10–12 hours. This soaking makes the rhubarb much easier to pack in the jars.

Using a slotted spoon, take the rhubarb from the syrup and pack into warm, sterilised jars (see p.160). Bring the syrup to the boil again and pour over the rhubarb, filling the jars to the brim. Cover with lids, remembering to loosen screw-bands, if you're using them, by a quarter of a turn (see p.164). Stand in a pan with a folded tea towel on the base. Cover the jars with warm water (at 38°C). Bring to simmering point (88°C) over a period of 25 minutes. Simmer at this temperature for 2 minutes.

Carefully remove the jars from the pan and place on a wooden surface or a folded tea towel. Tighten screw-bands. Leave undisturbed to cool for 24 hours then check the seals before storing. Use within a year.

Variation

Instead of honey and orange, try using 50g very finely sliced fresh root ginger and liven up the syrup with ginger cordial or, better still, some ginger wine. Both natives of Asia, ginger and rhubarb are natural partners. So often ingredients that coincide, seasonally or locally, complement each other in the culinary world.

Blues and bay

Season: late July to September

This recipe, applying the oven method, can be used for bottling the many members of the *Vaccinium* family, which include the cultivated blueberry as well as the wild bilberry (also known as whortleberry, whinberry or blaeberry, depending on your region). These bushy plants can be found growing wild on heath and moorland in many parts of Britain. The cultivated blueberry also thrives in the acidic soil of coastal east Dorset, as well as other parts of the country, and it is now possible to buy excellent English-grown 'blues' (see the directory, p.210). The delicate, lemony nutmeg note of fresh bay complements their gentle flavour beautifully.

Serve these fragrant berries for a breakfast treat with thick vanilla yoghurt.

Makes 3 x 500ml jars

150g caster sugar
50ml lemon juice (about ½ lemon)

1kg blueberries or bilberries
6 fresh bay leaves

Preheat the oven to 150°C/Gas Mark 2.

Start by making a fruit syrup: mix the sugar with 600ml water in a pan and bring slowly to the boil to dissolve the sugar. Remove from the heat, add the lemon juice, cover and keep warm.

Pick over the berries, removing any twiggy bits or leaves. Pack them firmly, without crushing, into warm, sterilised jars (see p.160), sliding the bay leaves attractively around the side of the jars.

Bring the sugar syrup to the boil and pour over the blueberries, filling the jars to the brim. Cover with lids, but do not fasten the clips or put on the screw-bands. Put the jars, 5cm apart, in the oven for 30 minutes.

Carefully remove the jars, seal with screw-bands or clips immediately and place on a wooden surface, newspaper or folded cloth. Leave undisturbed until completely cool and check the seal the following day.

Bottled blackcurrants

Season: June to August

The rich, intense flavour of blackcurrants is well preserved by bottling and I find it very useful to have a few jars on the larder shelf. Bottled currants are delicious served with hot steaming custard, vanilla ice cream or good plain yoghurt. When friends drop by, I often open a jar for an instant pud.

Makes 2 x 500ml jars
200g granulated sugar
1kg large, firm, juicy blackcurrants

A few lemon verbena or scented geranium leaves (optional)

Put the sugar into a pan with 600ml water and heat gently to dissolve, then boil for 1 minute to make a syrup.

Prepare the blackcurrants by removing any twiggy stalks and rinsing the fruit if necessary. Pack the currants as tightly as possible, but without crushing, into warm, sterilised jars (see p.160). If using verbena or geranium leaves, layer 2 or 3 amongst the little purple-black fruits as you go.

Cover the packed fruit with the hot syrup (at 60°C), filling the jars to the brim. Fasten with screw-bands or clips. If using screw-bands, remember to tighten them and then release by a quarter of a turn (see p.164). Place a folded tea towel in the bottom of a large pan (which must be deeper than your jars are tall). Fill the pan with warm water (at 38°C) then submerge the jars completely.

Clip a sugar thermometer to the side of the pan. Bring the water slowly to simmering point (88°C) over 25 minutes, then maintain this temperature for just 2 minutes.

Lift the jars out and place on a wooden surface or a folded tea towel. Tighten screw-bands. Leave undisturbed for 24 hours. To check they are properly sealed, remove the clips or screw-bands and lift the jars by their lids. Store in a cool, dark place. Use within a year.

Roasted tomato passata

For me, tomato passata is an essential store cupboard ingredient. I use it as a base for my roasted tomato ketchup (see p.195), as well as for pasta sauces and curries.

The best time to make this preserve is in August or September, when British tomatoes are at their cropping peak – smelling strong, sweet and aromatic when picked from the vine. This recipe uses 2kg fruit but, if you are using bought tomatoes as opposed to home-grown ones, I suggest you negotiate a good deal with your local grower and buy a boxful or two. You certainly won't regret it. You can't buy passata like this one!

Makes 2 x 500ml jars

2kg ripe tomatoes
200g shallots, peeled and thinly sliced
3–4 garlic cloves, peeled and
    thinly sliced
A few rosemary, thyme, basil
    or oregano sprigs

1 tsp salt
½ tsp ground black pepper
1 tsp sugar
50ml olive, sunflower or rapeseed oil

Preheat the oven to 180°C/Gas Mark 4.

Cut the tomatoes in half and place them, cut side up, in a single layer in a large roasting pan. Scatter the shallots, garlic, herbs, salt, pepper, sugar and oil over the top. Roast for about 1 hour, or until they are well softened. Remove from the oven and rub the tomatoes through a nylon sieve, or purée with a passata machine or mouli (see p.41).

Have your hot, sterilised jars ready (see p.160). Put the tomato purée into a saucepan and bring to boiling point. Pour it into the jars, filling them to the brim, and seal immediately with caps, clips or screw-bands. If you're using screw-bands, remember to release the lid by a quarter of a turn (see p.164).

Stand the jars in a large saucepan with a folded tea towel on the base. Cover with warm water and bring to simmering point (88°C) over a period of 25 minutes, then simmer for 10 minutes.

Remove the jars and stand them on a wooden surface or folded tea towel. Tighten the screw-bands, if using. Leave undisturbed until cold, then check the seal. Use within 12 months. Once opened, refrigerate and use within a few days.

Mulled pears

Season: late August to October

It always amazes me just how much fruit a gnarled old pear tree can bear in a good season. However, it's still a little tricky to catch pears at their point of perfect ripeness – somewhere between bullet hard and soft and woolly. Never mind, should you find yourself with a boxful of under-ripe specimens, this recipe turns them into a preserve 'pear excellence'.

These pears are particularly delicious served with thick vanilla custard, or used as a base for a winter fruit salad. Alternatively, try serving them with terrines and pâtés, or mix with chicory leaves drizzled with a honey mustard dressing and crumbly blue cheese.

Makes 2 x 1 litre jars
125g granulated sugar
500ml cider (dry, medium or sweet)
1.5kg small pears

Small handful of cloves
2 x 5cm pieces of cinnamon stick

Preheat the oven to 150°C/Gas Mark 2.

Start by making a cider syrup: mix the sugar with 500ml water in a pan and bring slowly to the boil to dissolve the sugar. Remove from the heat, add the cider, cover and keep warm.

Peel the pears, keeping the stalks attached. As you do so, place them in a bowl of lightly salted water to stop them browning. When all the pears are peeled, cut them in half and stud each half with a clove or two. Pack them into warm, sterilised jars (see p.160), adding a piece of cinnamon to each. Pears are very bottom-heavy of course, and I find the best way to pack them is head-to-toe.

Bring the cider syrup to the boil and pour over the pears. Cover the jars with lids, but do not fasten the clips or put on the screw-bands. Place the jars 5cm apart, in the oven, for 1 hour.

Remove the jars, seal with the screw-bands or clips immediately and place on a wooden surface, newspaper or folded cloth. Leave undisturbed until completely cool and check the seal the following day. Keep for up to 12 months.

Variation
Try replacing the cider with red wine and add a star anise to each jar if you like.

Spiced brandy plums

Season: August to early October

The Brogdale Trust in Kent is home to the National Fruit Collection – a bit like a Noah's Ark for the fruits of the earth. Among their many living specimens, they grow over 300 different cultivars of *Prunus domestica,* the European plum – also known as dessert plums. These fruits crop from high summer right through into October, giving us plenty to eat fresh, and loads to preserve for later in the year.

One of our great national fruits, plums are grown all over Britain and are often easy to find at farmer's markets and roadside stalls. So even if you miss the Early Rivers of late July, and you're away on holiday for the August Victorias, you should still be able to catch the Marjorie's Seedlings in September. Or you can bottle peaches, nectarines or apricot halves in the same way.

Makes 2 x 500ml jars

100g honey	1kg plums, stalks removed
Finely grated zest of 1 orange	2 cinnamon sticks
100ml brandy	2 star anise

Start by making a brandy syrup: put the honey and 400ml water into a pan, heat gently until the honey is dissolved, then add the orange zest and brandy. Set aside.

Halve the plums lengthwise with a sharp knife. Twist them apart and remove the stone with the point of the knife. Pack the plums into warmed, sterilised jars (see p.160) with the rounded sides of the fruit following the curve of the jar (you'll fit more in this way). Prod a cinnamon stick and a star anise down the side of each jar.

Pour the hot brandy syrup (at 60°C) over the fruit until the jars are full to the brim. Tap to remove any air bubbles. Seal with clips or screw-bands, remembering to release the screw-band by a quarter of a turn, if using this type of jar (see p.164).

Choose a large pan, deep enough for your jars to sit in and be totally immersed in water. Put a folded tea towel on the base and fill with warm water (at 38°C). Put the jars into the pan, making sure they are completely covered with the water. Bring to simmering point (88°C) over a period of 25 minutes, then maintain this temperature for 20 minutes.

Transfer the jars to a wooden surface or place on a folded tea towel. Tighten the screw-bands, if using. Leave undisturbed for 24 hours then check the seal is secure. Use within a year.

Figpote

Season: August to September

The fig is a member of the mulberry family and generally best suited to warmer climates than our own. However, a contented, well-positioned home-grown tree can still crop well, usually in August. In addition, September is peak season for imported figs, and they should be inexpensive and widely available. There are countless varieties, ranging in colour from purply-black to yellowy-green – any can be used for this recipe. Just make sure, when picking or buying, that your figs are ripe, as they do not ripen after picking.

This recipe uses a simplified version of the oven method. Everything is cooked and hot to start with, so it's not necessary to heat the jars for an extended time in the oven. A few jars of these honey-soaked fruits, stored away for the winter months, will be a blissful reminder that the hot days of summer were not just a fig-ment of your imagination...

Makes 2 x 250ml jars
12 figs (not too big)
150ml freshly squeezed orange juice

450ml Earl Grey tea or green tea
125g honey

Preheat the oven to 140°C/Gas Mark 1 and put your sterilised jars (see p.160) inside to heat.

Wash the figs and remove any hard, twiggy bits of stalk – but do not cut right back to the flesh, as this risks splitting the skin.

Put the orange juice, tea and honey into a pan and gently heat to simmering point to make a syrup. Add the figs and cook gently for 8–10 minutes, or until tender. Using a slotted spoon, take out the figs and carefully pack them into the hot jars (see p.164). It may be a bit of a squash, but figs quite like this. Return the filled jars to the oven to keep warm – it is important to keep the jars as hot as possible to create a successful seal.

Bring the fruit syrup to the boil and boil for 6–7 minutes to reduce it in volume. Stand the jars on a wooden surface or some newspaper and pour the hot syrup over the figs, filling the jars to the brim. Seal immediately with lids, clips or screw-bands. Leave undisturbed for 24 hours, then check the seal is secure. Use within a year.

Winter fruit compote

Season: winter

It may seem somewhat unnecessary to bottle dried fruit but I love having a few jars of this compote on the shelf. The once shrivelled fruits become plump and luscious and are quite delicious served alone for breakfast, or with yogurt or crème fraîche as a pudding.

I like to make this in early November, when newly dried prunes, figs and apricots are available. Keep a lookout for small, dried wild figs, which will plump up perfectly to their original shapely selves. The glistening black prunes from the Agen area in southern France are also key players – I prefer to use these unstoned because they infuse the compote with their almond-like essence. A handful of full-flavoured, unsulphured, sun-dried apricots complete the mix.

A simplified version of the oven method is used – everything is cooked and hot to start with, so the jars don't need to be heated for an extended time in the oven.

Makes 4 x 500ml jars
1 litre freshly made green tea, Earl Grey or breakfast tea
400g dried figs
200g unsulphured dried apricots
400g dried prunes, Agen prunes if possible, preferably with stones
200ml freshly squeezed orange juice
150g honey

Put the kettle on and make a large pot of tea (this is not for you, it's for the compote).

Combine the dried fruit in a large bowl. Pour the hot tea and orange juice over it and mix together, making sure all the fruit is totally immersed. Cover and leave to steep for 24 hours.

Preheat the oven to 140°C/Gas Mark 1 and place your sterilised jars (see p.160) inside. Carefully turn the fruit and liquid into a large pan. Bring slowly to simmering point and poach the fruit for 10 minutes.

Remove the pan of fruit from the heat. Using a slotted spoon, scoop out the fruit and pack into the hot jars. Return the jars to the oven to keep warm. Add the honey to the tea/orange steeping juice. Bring to the boil and boil for 5 minutes.

Carefully remove the jars from the oven and pour in the honeyed fruit juice so it comes to the very brim of the jars and completely covers the fruit. Seal immediately with lids, clips or screw-bands. Leave undisturbed for 24 hours, then check the seal is secure. Store in a cool, dry place and use within 12 months.

Liz's luscious raspberries

Season: July to late October

This recipe comes from Liz Neville, a virtuoso preserves maker with whom I run the River Cottage Preserved courses. You can make it with any raspberry, but we particularly like to use the big autumn berries which generously stretch the soft-fruit season well into October, even November. Bottle a few and you can extend your raspberry eating well into the dark winter months.

In an ideal world, the fruit for this preserve would be packed into the jars as you pick it from the canes. That may not be possible – but do make sure the fruit is in tip-top condition and handled as little as possible.

Makes 3 x 500ml jars
150g granulated sugar
1kg firm, just-ripe raspberries

100–150ml brandy, gin, vodka or raspberry liqueur

First make a syrup: put the sugar and 750ml water into a pan and heat slowly to dissolve the sugar then bring to the boil. Keep the syrup warm.

Pack the raspberries tightly into warm, sterilised jars (see p.160). Make sure you don't bruise the fruit – a chopstick or wooden spoon handle is useful for gently prodding it down. Pour the alcohol over the packed fruit. Fill the jars to the brim with the sugar syrup, tapping them to remove any air bubbles. Put the lids on the jars, loosening screw-bands by a quarter of a turn, if you're using them, to allow the steam to escape (see p.164).

Stand the jars in a deep pan and cover with warm water (at 38°C). Heat to simmering point (88°C), over 25 minutes. Maintain this temperature for 2 minutes.

Carefully remove the jars and stand them on a wooden surface or thick folded towel. Tighten the screw-bands then leave the jars undisturbed to cool. When cold, check the seal by removing the clips or screw-bands and lifting the jar by the lid. Use within 12 months.

Quince and apple sauce

Season: September to October

The raw flesh of the lumpy yellow quince is dry and disagreeably sour. However, once cooked, it becomes pink and highly perfumed. Lightly sweetened and combined with good fluffy cooking apples, such as Bramleys, it makes a delightful accompaniment for roast pork or duck. I also love this aromatic fruity sauce on a home-baked rice pudding.

Makes 4 x 250ml jars

500g quince, peeled, cored and chopped

Juice of ½ lemon

500g cooking apples, peeled, cored and chopped

125g granulated sugar

Put the quince, lemon juice and 500ml water into a saucepan. Bring to the boil then simmer for 8–10 minutes (quince takes longer to soften than apple and needs a bit of a head start). Add the apples and sugar and cook for a further 10–15 minutes until all the fruit is well softened. Remove from the heat and either beat to a smooth pulp with a wooden spoon or rub through a sieve.

Meanwhile, preheat the oven to 140°C/Gas Mark 1 and place your sterilised jars (see p.160) inside.

Return the pulp to the pan and bring to the boil, stirring to make sure it doesn't catch and burn. Remove from the heat and pour immediately into the warm, sterilised jars. Seal with lids, clips or screw-bands, remembering to release the screw-band by a quarter of a turn if using this type of jar (see p.164). Place in a deep pan with a folded tea towel on the bottom. Cover with warm water, bring to simmering point (88°C), then simmer for 5 minutes.

Remove the jars from the hot water and place on a wooden surface or folded tea towel. Tighten the screw-bands, if using, and leave the jars undisturbed until cold. Check the seal. Store in a cool, dry place. Use within 12 months.

Sauces, Ketchups & Oil-based Preserves

Sauces, pastes and condiments are among the tasty

recipes in this chapter. Vinegar, sugar, salt and oil all come into play as preservatives; you will find more detailed information on these ingredients on pp.35–9. Oil has been used as an air-excluding ingredient since ancient times to keep foods from spoiling, but it is not a common preserving medium in this country. However, with the increasing availability of superb-quality oils, produced both here and abroad, this delicious and luxurious way of preserving is becoming much more accessible. It is certainly a branch of preserving that I find very exciting and rewarding.

This chapter will introduce you to the following range of preserves:

Sauces This is a generic term if ever there was one, but for the purposes of this book, I define a sauce as a smooth condiment generally made with similar ingredients to a chutney (see p.94). The cooked, spiced fruits and vegetables are either sieved or puréed to give a thick, pourable consistency.

Ketchups Sometimes referred to in old recipe books as 'catsups' or 'catchups', these are generally thinner than sauces and made from a single fruit or vegetable with vinegar and seasonings.

Vegetables in oil The technique of using oil to preserve lightly blanched or brined vegetables is strongly associated with Mediterranean countries, where olive oil is abundant. It is particularly suited to vegetables with strong flavours, such as globe artichokes, asparagus, dried tomatoes and mushrooms – not least because they will flavour the oil, which can also be used.

Pesto and pastes These intense condiments are made from aromatic or strongly spiced ingredients and do not contain high levels of salt, vinegar or other preservatives. For this reason, they need to be sealed off from the air with a layer of oil, refrigerated, and generally should not be kept for more than a month or two. After some has been taken from the jar, the oil covering should always be replaced, which may mean topping up with a little more.

Flavoured oils Easily made by steeping herbs, spices or other robustly flavoured ingredients in oil, these are among the simplest and most rewarding of preserves to make. They enliven everything from salad dressings and mayonnaise to marinades and stir-fries. Use warm oil for firm ingredients such as chillies and spices, and cold oil for green herbs.

Coulis Made from very lightly sweetened fruit that is simply sieved or puréed, coulis are usually based on juicy summer berries and currants.

Garden pesto

Season: July to August

The big, plate-like leaves of the nasturtium plant (*Tropaeolum majus*) are abundant throughout the summer, and often well into the golden months of autumn. With their peppery flavour, they make the perfect base for a fiery pesto. Add a sprig or two of garden mint, a few golden marigold petals and some spicy nasturtium seeds and you have a wonderful sauce to stir into pasta, swirl on soups or just smear in a sandwich. Pick the leaves on a warm, dry day – ideally earlier in the summer, before the caterpillars have decided to feast on them.

Whenever I make pesto, I replace the traditional Parmesan with a local goat's cheese called Capriano. Made by Dorset-based Woolsery Cheese (see the directory, p.210), this is a hard goat's cheese, matured for a year. It makes an excellent alternative to Parmesan in all kinds of dishes. Using home-produced hemp oil instead of olive oil is another way to make your pesto more home-grown. If you find the pungent flavour of hemp oil a little too strong, you can combine it or replace it with rapeseed oil. See the directory for more details.

Makes 2 x 225g jars

50g nasturtium leaves
2–3 mint leaves (optional)
2 garlic cloves, peeled and crushed
6 or so nasturtium seed pods
    (see p.111)
50g pine nuts (optional)
75g mature, hard goat's cheese
    or Parmesan, finely grated

Juice of ½ lemon (50ml)
150ml hemp, rapeseed or olive oil,
    plus extra to seal
Petals from 2 marigold flowers
Salt to taste

Purists say that pesto should be made by pounding the ingredients together using a pestle and mortar. For this recipe, you can certainly do that, starting by crushing the mint leaves, garlic, nasturtium seeds and nuts, then adding the cheese, followed by the lemon juice and oil. Pound until well blended, folding in the marigold petals and salt at the very end.

Then again, you can do as I do and simply whiz everything (except the marigold petals and salt) in a food processor for a couple of minutes until you have a soft, well-blended mixture. Remove from the processor, and fold in the petals and salt.

(continued overleaf)

Either way, spoon the pesto into small, sterilised jars (see p.29) and pour a little oil over the surface to exclude any air. Cap with metal lids. Store in the fridge and use within 4 weeks. If you are making a lot of pesto, pack in small containers and freeze.

When you come to use the pesto, stir it well before spooning out. Make sure the surface of any pesto remaining in the jar is completely covered with oil before you return it to the fridge (this is very important if it is to keep well).

Variations

Traditionally, pesto is made with the leaves of the sweet basil plant (*Ocimum basilicum*). It's better suited to warmer climates than ours, where there are fewer slugs to devour the sweetly pungent leaves, but, if you manage to grow it in good quantities, do make use of it in this recipe. Alternatively, try some of our native herbs as the base for your pesto. Young, raw nettle tops and wild garlic leaves (both to be gathered in early spring) work beautifully together, as does parsley (flat leaf or curly). Hazels or walnuts can stand in for pine nuts, and a mature, robust Cheddar is a good alternative to Parmesan.

P.S. *Calendula officinalis*, or common garden marigold, is a really useful herb and should not to be ignored for culinary purposes. The golden pigment of the petals can be used, like saffron, to colour rice, cakes, desserts and butter. Alternatively, sprinkle the bittersweet, aromatic petals over mixed salad leaves, or toss a few into a fresh herb omelette.

Slow-dried tomatoes in oil

Season: July to September

I love the gutsy flavour of these tomatoes and like to serve them as part of a crisp smoked bacon and beetroot salad, or a hearty couscous salad with plenty of fresh coriander. There are times though, when I can't resist eating them from the jar!

Ideally the fruit would be sun-dried but we just don't have sufficient hours of sunshine in this country. Slowly drying them in a very low oven achieves similar and very pleasing results, although you do need a sizeable quantity of tomatoes.

Makes 2–3 x 225g jars

2kg tomatoes
2 tsp salt
2 tsp granulated sugar

100ml white wine vinegar
200–300ml olive, rapeseed
    or sunflower oil

Preheat the oven to 100°C/Gas Mark ¼. Cut the tomatoes in half around their middles and scoop out the pips with a teaspoon. Put the tomatoes, cut side up, on a wire rack with a baking sheet underneath to catch any drips. Sprinkle a few grains of salt and sugar on each cut tomato half. Leave for 10–15 minutes for the seasoning to begin to permeate the tomato flesh, then turn the tomatoes so their cut sides face down on the rack.

Set the rack of tomatoes over the baking sheet in the oven and leave them to dry for 6–10 hours; the drying time will depend on their size and juiciness. The tomatoes are ready when they are dry to the touch but still a little plump and fleshy. They'll have reduced by around 90 per cent and the total weight after drying will be about 200g. Don't let the tomatoes dry until they become brittle. Remove from the oven and allow to cool, then transfer to a shallow dish. Pour the vinegar over the tomatoes, cover and leave to stand for about 30 minutes.

Pack the tomatoes into sterilised jars (see p.29) to within 2cm of the top of the jar. Distribute the vinegar between the jars and then cover the tomatoes completely with oil, tapping the jar to expel any trapped air. Seal with lids. Store in a cool, dry place and use within 4 months. Once opened, store in the fridge, always make sure the tomatoes are fully covered with oil, and use within 6 weeks.

Variations

Use half balsamic and half white wine vinegar if you prefer. A tablespoonful or two of finely chopped preserved lemons is a flavourful addition.

Roasted tomato ketchup

Season: July to September

Slow-roasted tomatoes provide a rich, intense base for this, my all-time favourite ketchup. The spices and seasonings I have used are good old-fashioned ones – those our grandmothers would have kept in their kitchens. However, if you like, you can fire it up by adding a couple of teaspoonfuls of chilli powder. Don't expect the ketchup to be the same colour as a commercial variety; it will be a warm orangey-red colour.

Makes 500–600ml

1 quantity (1 litre) roast tomato
    passata (see p.173)
100ml cider vinegar
50ml lemon juice
1 heaped tsp celery salt

1 heaped tsp mustard powder
1 heaped tsp ground ginger
½ tsp ground black pepper
¼ tsp ground cloves
100g demerara sugar

Put the passata into a heavy-based pan with the vinegar, lemon juice and spices. Bring to simmering point then add the sugar. Stir until dissolved then continue to simmer, stirring occasionally, for 25–30 minutes, until the sauce is reduced to a thick but pourable consistency.

Pour immediately into warm, sterilised bottles or jars (see p.160). Seal immediately with vinegar-proof lids. Store in a cool, dry place and use within 4 months. For longer keeping, sterilise the filled jars using the method on p.133. Once opened, keep in the fridge.

Variation

Rhubarb makes a delightful fruity ketchup and is a good way to use up the tougher, tarter stalks towards the end of the rhubarb season. Slow roast 2kg chopped rhubarb with 250g chopped red onions and 3–4 garlic cloves at 180°C/Gas Mark 4 for about an hour. Sieve the mixture and put into a heavy-based saucepan. Use the same quantities of sugar and vinegar as above, but leave out the lemon juice (as rhubarb is very acidic). Replace the mustard, black pepper and cloves with a good teaspoonful each of ground cumin and coriander. Continue to cook as for tomato ketchup.

Harissa paste

Season: July to September

Harissa is a North African ingredient, used to enhance many fish and meat dishes, as well as couscous and soups. I also like to use my version to make a fruity, fiery dipping sauce (see below) to serve with pork, fish or prawns.

The strength of the paste depends on the variety and quantity of chillies used. The chances are that this recipe, which I would describe as moderately hot, will merely tickle the palate of out-and-out chilli freaks. But all you need do, to make it fierier, is increase the amount of chillies, include more of their seeds (see below), or perhaps add one or two very hot little dried chillies.

Makes 2 x 112g jars

250g tomatoes
50g hot chillies
2 fat garlic cloves
50g shallots

1 tsp caraway seeds
1 tsp coriander seeds
½ tsp salt
50ml olive or hemp oil

Drop the tomatoes into a pan of boiling water for 30 seconds then scoop out and peel off the skins.

Remove the stalk and calyx from the chillies. The seeds contain most of the fruit's heat and, at this point, you can choose either to leave all the seeds in or, for a less intense paste, cut at least some of them out. Either way, make sure you wash your hands after handling chillies and avoid touching your eyes for a while, as the chilli oil will burn them.

Put the skinned tomatoes, chillies and all the other ingredients, except the oil, in a food processor and blitz until well blended. Tip into a small saucepan and heat until boiling then simmer for about 10 minutes until reduced and starting to thicken. Leave to cool. Pack into warm, sterilised jars (see p.29), leaving a 1cm gap at the top. Pour oil over the paste to completely cover it. Seal the jars.

Store in the fridge and use within 4 months. If you want to extend the shelf life, pack in small, sealable containers and freeze. Once opened, keep in the fridge, making sure the paste in the jar is completely covered by a layer of oil.

P.S. For a tasty chilli plum dipping sauce, simmer 50ml rice or cider vinegar, 100g plum jam (see p.69) and 1 tsp harissa paste until reduced and thickened.

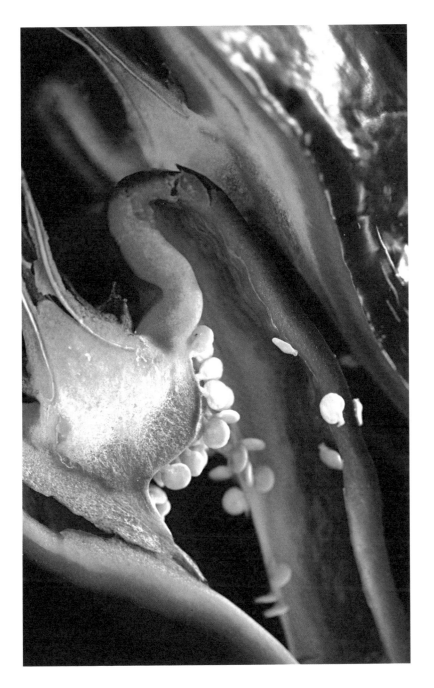

Asparagus preserved in oil

Season: May to June

Spotting the first tips of asparagus pushing their way above ground in late spring is one of the greatest moments of the growing year. It means there will be asparagus to eat every day for the next few weeks; I also like to preserve a few jarfuls.

Use a good, but not really expensive olive oil (see p.39). When the asparagus has been eaten, the flavoured oil can be used to make a lovely salad dressing.

You will need one jam jar, about 20cm high, with a capacity of around 500ml, and a second jar of 250ml capacity.

Makes 2 jars (1 x 500ml, 1 x 250ml)

500g asparagus
300ml cider vinegar or
   white wine vinegar
2 fat garlic cloves or shallots,
   finely sliced

1 tsp peppercorns
A few rosemary, thyme or
   basil sprigs
100ml lemon juice
400–500ml olive oil

Trim away the tough woody ends of the asparagus, then cut into lengths 1cm less than the height of your larger jar, keeping the tender trimmed-off bits to one side.

Put the vinegar and 200ml water in a saucepan and bring to the boil. Remove from the heat and cover to keep warm. Meanwhile, place a griddle pan over a high heat. Add the long asparagus spears and cook, turning once or twice, until lightly charred. Drop the spears into the hot vinegar bath and leave for 3–4 minutes. This sharpens the flavour of the asparagus, while the acidity assists in preventing bacterial growth.

Put about two-thirds of the garlic or shallot and peppercorns in the sterilised 500ml jar. Remove the asparagus from the vinegar bath and pack it, upright, into the jar. Add a few herbs. Pour over two-thirds of the lemon juice, then cover completely with oil. Seal with a lid. Repeat the entire process with the trimmed-off ends in the smaller jar, using up the remaining peppercorns, garlic, herbs, lemon juice and oil.

Keep in a cool, dark place for 6 weeks before using. Consume within 4 months. Once opened, keep in the fridge, making sure the asparagus in the jar remains covered with oil, and use within 6 weeks.

Variations
Substitute char-grilled peppers or lightly cooked artichoke hearts for the asparagus.

Flavoured oils

Season: more or less any time

These are dead easy to make and have endless applications in the kitchen. Use them to baste or brown ingredients and they will add pizzazz and excitement to stews and roasts. Likewise, they will jazz up a panful of onions or other veg for a soup or sauce, and impart character to fish dishes. Herb oils come into their own when drizzled over summer or winter salads; they are also excellent used in mayonnaises and dressings.

The basic principle is to choose robust flavourings and leave them for long enough to impart their mighty characters to the oil. Always use a good-quality oil as your base (see pp.38–9). In all cases, to prevent the oil becoming rancid, store in a cool place and use within 6 months.

Chilli oil
Split open 6–8 dried or fresh chillies. Pack into a dry, sterilised 500–600ml jar or bottle (see p.160), along with 1 tsp black peppercorns. Heat 500ml olive or rapeseed oil to about 40°C and pour over the chillies. Cover and leave to infuse for 14 days – a little more for a stronger oil. Strain and re-bottle.

Nice spice oil
In a dry frying pan, heat 1 tbsp each of coriander, cumin and fennel seeds together with a couple of dried chillies. Toast until they release their distinctive fragrances and just start to brown – shake the pan frequently to prevent them from burning. Crush the toasted seeds then transfer them to a dry, sterilised 500–600ml jar or bottle (see p.160). Pour over 500ml rapeseed oil. Leave for a couple of weeks before straining the oil and re-bottling.

Herb oil
Lightly pack a dry, sterilised 580ml jar (see p.160) with freshly gathered herbs such as basil, rosemary, thyme, sage or oregano. You can use individual herbs on their own or mix a few together. Pour over 500ml olive oil and leave in a cool place for a couple of weeks before straining and re-bottling the oil.

Pontack (elderberry) sauce

Season: August to September

This is kitchen alchemy at its most exciting and rewarding: a mysterious-looking brew of dark elderberries, vinegar and spices becomes a truly wonderful sauce, a secret weapon for the store cupboard that I don't like to be without. According to tradition, pontack sauce is best used after 7 years, but I'm hard pushed to keep it for 7 months. Pungent, fruity and spicy, it's an unrivalled partner for winter stews, casseroled liver, slow-roasted belly of pork, or anything wild and gamey. Besides serving this sauce alongside meat dishes, you can add a couple of tablespoonfuls to sauces and gravies.

The elderberry season is short and the berries are part of the hedgerow banquet for woodland birds, so don't delay – gather when you see them.

Makes 1 x 350ml bottle

500g elderberries
500ml cider vinegar
200g shallots, peeled and sliced
6 cloves

4 allspice berries
1 blade of mace
1 tbsp black peppercorns
15g fresh root ginger, bruised

Strip the berries from the stalks as soon as possible after picking – a table fork is useful for doing this. Place them in an ovenproof earthenware or glass dish with the vinegar and put in a very low oven (about 130°C/Gas Mark ½) for 4–6 hours, or overnight. Remove from the oven and strain through a sieve, crushing the berries with a potato masher as you do so, to obtain maximum juice.

Put the rich, red-black juice in the pan along with the sliced shallots, spices and ginger. Bring gently to the boil and cook for 20–25 minutes until slightly reduced (perhaps muttering some magic charm while you watch over the dark, bubbling potion). Remove from the heat and strain through a sieve.

Return the juice to the pan and bring to the boil, then boil steadily for 5 minutes. Pour the sauce into a warm, sterilised bottle (see p.160) and seal. Store in a cool, dark cupboard.

P.S. This sauce grows better with age, so try to lay some bottles down for a few months if you can.

Saucy haw ketchup

Season: September to December

Hawthorn is widespread throughout Britain, and frequently used for hedging along farmland or roads. It's a lovely tree and provides vital natural accommodation for native birds, insects and invertebrates. Frothy white hawthorn blossom heralds the beginning of summer and the fading flowers later give way to developing clusters of blood-red berries, or haws. These swathe the hedgerows from early autumn well into winter – sometimes even through to the new year. The peppery, lemony little berries are too tart to eat raw, but I love them cooked into this sweet-sour hedgerow sauce.

Hawthorn tends to fruit prolifically, so you should have little trouble gathering enough haws. Do avoid picking from roadside bushes, however, as these may have absorbed fumes and pollution (although, for some reason, they often seem to be laden with the biggest and juiciest berries of all!).

Serve haw ketchup with rich meats such as venison or slow-roast belly of pork. It is also terrific drizzled over Welsh rarebit. My favourite way to enjoy this spicy sauce, however, is with a really good nut roast, served with a crisp green salad.

Makes 1 x 300ml bottle
500g haws
300ml white wine vinegar or
   cider vinegar

170g sugar
½ tsp salt
Ground black pepper to taste

Strip the haws from the stalks – the easiest way to do this is to snip them off with a pair of scissors or secateurs. Rinse in cold water.

Put the haws into a pan with the vinegar and 300ml water and simmer for about 30 minutes – the skins will split, revealing the firm, yellow flesh. Cook until the flesh is soft and the berries have become a muted red-brown. Remove from the heat. Rub the mixture through a sieve, or pass through a food mill, to remove the largish stones and the skins.

Return the fruity mixture to the cleaned-out pan. Add the sugar and heat gently, stirring, until it dissolves. Bring to the boil and cook for 5 minutes. Season with the salt and pepper. Pour into a sterilised bottle (see p.160) and seal with a vinegar-proof cap. Use within 12 months.

Souper mix

Season: more or less any time

A good vegetable bouillon or stock can be the making of many a soup, risotto or sauce. Preparing your own stock from scratch is easy enough – but it does take a little time, so an instant alternative is often welcome. The choice of vegetable bouillon powders and stock cubes on the market is pretty limited. There are one or two good products but, if you use them frequently, you might find an underlying uniformity creeping into your cooking. This is my solution. Whip up your very own souper mix – a concentrated paste of fresh vegetables simply preserved with salt. It's quick and easy to make and the stock it produces is delicious.

You can use just about any herb or vegetable you like – the important thing is that they are fresh and taste as *vegetabley* as possible. My preferred ingredients are indicated in this recipe, but you could also use young turnips, shallots, celery, swede, beetroot or peppers, as well as bay, thyme, lovage or mint – almost anything, really. Just bear in mind that the character of the stock will vary depending on the ingredients you choose.

The following are prepared weights, i.e. the ingredients should be washed, trimmed and peeled (where necessary).

Makes 3 x 340g jars

250g leek	2–3 garlic cloves
200g fennel	100g parsley
200g carrot	100g coriander
250g celeriac	250g salt
50g sun-dried tomatoes	

The helping hand of a food processor is essential in this recipe. Simply put all the ingredients into the processor and blend together. The result will be a moist, granular paste. Spoon into sterilised jars (see p.29) and seal with vinegar-proof lids.

Keep one jar of the mix in the fridge – within easy reach for everyday cooking. The rest can be stored in a cool, dark and dry place. Use within 6 months.

To use souper mix, just stir about 10g (2 tsp) of it into 500ml hot water.

Useful Things

Directory

Preserving equipment and jam jar stockists

Kilner Jars (new jars and refurbishment of old rings)
www.kilnerjarsuk.co.uk
01372 372611

Jam Jar Shop (jars, lids, labels and general preserving equipment)
www.jamjarshop.com
01572 720720

Soap Kitchen (paraffin wax for sealing fruit)
www.soapkitchenonline.co.uk
01805 622221

Just Preserving
www.justpreserving.co.uk
01692 405984

Ascott, The 'Good Life' Store
www.ascott.biz
0845 130 6285

Lakeland Ltd
www.lakeland.co.uk
01539 488100

Wares of Knutsford
www.waresofknutsford.co.uk
0845 612 1273

Note that glycerine and glucose syrup are available from most chemists

Specialist ingredient suppliers

Oldroyd & Sons Ltd (forced rhubarb)
www.yorkshirerhubarb.co.uk
0113 2822245

Trehane Nursery (English blueberries)
www.trehanenursery.co.uk
01202 873490

Mr Trollope of Fingringhoe (quinces and medlars by mail order)
01206 735405

The Garlic Farm on the Isle of Wight
www.thegarlicfarm.co.uk
01983 865378

Peppers by Post
www.peppersbypost.biz
01308 897766

South Devon Chilli Farm
www.sdcf.co.uk
01548 550782

Steenbergs (organic and fair trade spices and spice infusers)
www.steenbergs.co.uk
01765 640088

The Anglesey Sea Salt Company Ltd (Halen Môn salt)
www.seasalt.co.uk
01248 430871

Cornish Sea Salt
www.cornishseasalt.co.uk
0845 337 5277

Maldon Salt (sea and rock salt)
www.maldonsalt.co.uk
01621 853315

Aspall (organic cider vinegar)
www.aspall.co.uk
01728 860510

The Somerset Distillery (cider vinegar,
eau de vie and cider brandy)
www.ciderbrandy.co.uk
01460 240782

Woolsery Cheese (Capriano cheese)
www.woolserycheese.co.uk
01300 341991

R Oil (rapeseed oil)
www.r-oil.co.uk
01451 870387

Yorkshire Hemp (hemp oil)
www.yorkshirehemp.com
01924 375475

Good Oil (hemp oil)
www.goodwebsite.co.uk

Billingtons Sugar Ltd (unrefined,
fair trade and organic sugar)
www.billingtons.co.uk
01733 422368

Silver Spoon (English beet sugar
and jam sugar with pectin)
www.silverspoon.co.uk
01733 422696

Food festivals

The last few years have seen a move to
the organisation of many regional and
local food festivals as well as a
whopping increase in vibrant farmers'
and country markets around Britain.
These events provide a wonderful
opportunity to buy from local growers
and help keep rural communities alive.
This list comprises a number of annual
events, as well as organisations that link
into seasonal events and food diversity.

Apples

National Apple Day is 21 October.
Local events are held throughout the
country on or around this date – see
the charity Common Ground's website
for venues.
www.commonground.org.uk

Citrus fruits (for marmalade)

The world's original marmalade event is
held on the second weekend in February.
Marmalade Festival, Dalemain House,
Penrith, Cumbria
www.marmaladefestival.com

Damsons

Damson Day is held in Cumbria in the
middle of April, celebrating damson
blossom with various walks.
www.lythdamsons.co.uk

Pears

Pear Day is a September pear harvest
of the historic collection of pears at
Cannon Hall, near Barnsley.
www.barnsley.gov.uk
01226 790270

Plums

Pershore in Worcestershire hold a Plum Festival on August Bank Holiday.
www.pershoreplumfestival.org.uk

Rhubarb

A Spring Festival of Food, Drink and Rhubarb is held at the beginning of March.
www.wakefield.gov.uk

Asparagus

An opportunity for enthusiasts to taste and learn about this prize vegetable. Asparagus Festival, Pershore, Worcestershire
www.britishasparagusfestival.org

Chillies

Chichester holds a lively hot chilli festival in August.
www.westdean.org.uk

Garlic

The Isle of Wight Garlic Festival is an annual garlic harvest celebration held in the third week of August.
www.thegarlicfarm.co.uk

Associations and charities

British Beekeepers' Association (promoting bees and beekeeping)
www.britishbee.org.uk

Brogdale Horticultural Trust (home of the National Fruit Collection)
www.brogdale.org

Farm Retail Association (information on your local farm shop or pick-your-own farm)
www.farmshopping.com

National Association of Farmers' Markets (information on your nearest market)
www.farmersmarket.net

National Society of Allotment and Leisure Gardeners
www.nsalg.org.uk
01536 266576

The National Trust
www.nationaltrust.org.uk

Royal Horticultural Association (find your nearest horticultural group or club)
www.rhs.org.uk
0845 260 5000

Rural Revival
www.ruralrevival.org.uk

Soil Association (information on organic and local food)
www.soilassociation.org

Country Markets
www.country-markets.co.uk

Conversion charts

Metric quantities are given in the recipes. Use the following conversions if you prefer to work in imperial measures.

Weight

Metric	Imperial
25g	1oz
50g	2oz
100g–125g	4oz
170g	6oz
200g	7oz
225g	8oz
275g	10oz
340g	12oz
400g	14oz
450g	1lb
500g	1lb 2oz
900g	2lb
1kg	2lb 4oz

Liquid/volume

Metric	Imperial
150ml	5fl oz (¼ pint)
300ml	10fl oz (½ pint)
600ml	20fl oz (1 pint)
1 litre	35fl oz (1¾ pints)

1 tsp (1 teaspoon) = 5ml
1 tbsp (1 tablespoon) = 15ml

What is a gill? This old-fashioned term often crops up in old recipe books and one gill is equivalent to 150ml or ¼ pint.

Oven temperatures

	°C	°F	Gas Mark
Very cool	130	250	½
Very cool	140	275	1
Cool	150	300	2
Warm	160–170	325	3
Moderate	180	350	4
Fairly hot	190–200	375–400	5–6
Hot	210–220	425	7
Very hot	230–240	450–475	8–9

Acknowledgements

When asked if I would write this book, I hadn't realised just how many waking (and night-time) moments my thoughts would invariably be stuck in some form of jam jar or another. It's been a huge privilege, giving me the opportunity to adventure into new, exciting and often stirring territories, all contained in the amazing world of preserving. However, it would not have been possible for me to do so without the immeasurable help and support of family, friends and acquaintances, who have journeyed with me, solidly supporting me throughout.

First and foremost heartfelt thanks to Gavin Kingcome for his stunning photography, bringing ingredients and recipes alive, and for his steady patience on our photo-shoot days. Also to Nikki Duffy for her thoroughly attentive detail in checking recipes, thus reinforcing your success and victory in the jam pan.

Thank you to friends and neighbours in and around the Uplyme Valleys for their open generosity in allowing me to beg and sometimes steal produce from over the garden wall. I would particularly like to thank John and Henriette Wood for giving me a free rein to visit Rhode Hill Gardens – its rich bio-diversity quite the highlight of photo-shoot days.

On the technical front, thanks to Liz Neville for her invaluable fund of preserving knowledge, and to the outstanding technical team at Wilkin & Sons Ltd.

My thanks to the thoughtful and brilliant Bloomsbury team: Richard Atkinson, Natalie Hunt and Erica Jarnes; along with Will Webb for his outstanding work and ideas on the layout. Sincere thanks also to gifted editor Janet Illsley who meticulously and with great calm has perfectly potted, packed and sealed the book.

Thank you to Trisha Bye for keeping my kitchen and jam jars in apple pie order; and to her daughter Sophie for her jammy creativeness. Thanks also to Lois Wakeman for her 'on the spot' availability for eleventh hour photography.

At home, thank you to my husband Hugh for his support at all times, particularly for his lack of complaint when I dropped a full 2-litre bottle of his amazingly good sloe gin. To Pip and Maddy, who have never faltered with their help, advice and enthusiasm, and have seemingly always shared family life with a ton or two of jam.

A big thank you to Rob Love and the River Cottage team for their confidence that I could write the book. And last, but by no means least, immense thanks to Hugh F-W, warrior and leader of the *seasonal and local revolution* ... long may it last!

Index

River Cottage Handbooks

Seasonal, Local, Organic, Wild

FOR FURTHER INFORMATION AND
TO ORDER ONLINE, VISIT
RIVERCOTTAGE.NET